Victor Mollo

THE HOG

Takes To Precision

Collected and Edited by Mark Horton

Master Point Press • Toronto, Canada

Master Point Press
331 Douglas Ave.
Toronto, Ontario, Canada
M5M 1H2   (416)781-0351

Email: info@masterpointpress.com
Websites: www.masterpointpress.com
              www.masteringbridge.com
              www.bridgeblogging.com
              www.ebooksbridge.com

Library and Archives Canada Cataloguing in Publication

Mollo, Victor
The hog takes to precision / Victor Mollo.

Short stories.
Issued also in electronic formats.

ISBN 978-1-897106-66-2

1. Contract bridge--Fiction. I. Title.

PR6063.O43H65 2011   823'.914   C2010-906871-8

Editor   Ray Lee
Interior format   Sally Sparrow
Cover and interior design Olena S. Sullivan/New Mediatrix

1 2 3 4 5 6 7   15 14 13 12 11
PRINTED IN CANADA

Contents

Introduction		5
1.	The Hog Takes to Precision	11
2.	Teaching the Rabbit Precision	17
3.	Precision and the Money Motif	23
4.	The Play Is in the Bidding	29
5.	When in Doubt, Play Precision	35
6.	The Case Against Precision	39
7.	Precision in the Menagerie	45
8.	It's the Shock that Does the Damage	51
9.	Anyone Can Make a Mistake	59
10.	Sinning in Safety	65
11.	The Rabbit Counts up to Three	71
12.	Monster Points	75
13.	An Unholy Match	81
14.	The Hog and the Iced Water	85
15.	Madness in the Cards	93
16.	The Hog's Etiquette	101
17.	The Age of Chivalry	107
18.	Satanic Hands	113
19.	The Rabbit Discards the Queen of Trumps	115
20.	Monster Math	123
21.	Animal Law	131
22.	Small Slams in the Menagerie	137
23.	Memories in the Menagerie	143
24.	Bad Feelings in the Menagerie	151
25.	Brilliant Dummy Plays	159

26. THE GREEDY DOUBLE 165

27. THE RABBIT IN LOVE 173

28. CONCENTRATING ON THE IMPROBABLE 179

29. THE CARDS TAKE CHARGE 185

30. THE PAPADOPOULOS SCHOOL OF THOUGHT 191

31. A ONE-SIDED MATCH 197

32. THE IMPRESSIONIST SCHOOL OF BRIDGE 203

Introduction

Victor Mollo was born in St. Petersburg into a rich Russian family. When he was eight, the October Revolution occurred and his family fled Russia, traveling by a purchased train, with forged Red Cross papers, crossing into Finland, then Stockholm, Paris and finally London. He neglected his studies and devoted himself to bridge. As an editor in the European service of the British Broadcasting Corporation, he began to write books and articles on the game. After retirement in London in 1969, he started to write even more extensively, and during the time until his death in 1987 he wrote thirty books and hundreds of articles. He was also active in developing bridge cruises, mostly in the Mediterranean.

His lifestyle was exceptional. He would play rubber bridge at his club each afternoon, enjoy dinner and wine with his wife, the Squirrel, and then work all night until 6 a.m., when he would take a nap. While he occasionally successfully competed in the major duplicate bridge tournaments, winning four national titles, he preferred rubber bridge. Many of his daily achievements at the rubber bridge table would become elements in his fictional stories.

THE BRIDGE IN THE MENAGERIE SERIES

The *Bridge in the Menagerie* series started with the book of the same name, first published in 1965. Most of the pieces had previously appeared in either *Bridge Magazine* or the American *The Bridge World* and that pattern was repeated in the works that followed. Mollo was recognized as 'the most entertaining writer of the game' in a poll among American players in the 1980s. Although duplicate bridge features from time to time, the books largely focus on entertaining events at a rubber bridge table in the Griffins Club. Many of the characters are nicknamed after the animals that they most resemble both physically and psychologically, and that caricature common archetypes of real-life bridge players.

Mollo often refers to the main characters by their initials. They include:

H.H.   *'Please, please partner, let me play the hand. I assure you that it's in your own interest.'* Much the best player and the biggest bully, aptly named the Hideous Hog. Regarded as a genius, he cannot understand why he is so grossly underrated. His greatest rival is:

Papa   *'The essence of bridge is to see through the backs of the cards.'* Themistocles Papadopoulos — Papa the Greek — who alone among the Griffins challenges the Hog's supremacy. A fine technician, intuitive, so subtle is Papa that he can falsecard with a singleton. And he always knows what everyone will do — except that the Hog usually does something else.

Karapet   *'Again everything has happened to me.'* Karapet Djoulikyan, the Free Armenian (Karapet the Unlucky), is without doubt the unluckiest mortal since Job. He has come to expect the worst and is rarely disappointed. Worse still, no Griffin these days will listen to his hard luck stories, and one or two have even had the temerity to tell him their own.

R.R.   *'One gets used to abuse. It's waiting for it that is so trying.'* The Rueful Rabbit is gentle, generous, always ready to help — more especially his opponents. The Rabbit used to think of himself as the second-worst player in the world. But that was before he met the Toucan. R.R. rarely knows what he is doing or why he is doing it, but hovering over him is the best Guardian Angel in the business, and every time R.R. does something outrageously idiotic the Angel waves a magic wand and the ugly duckling turns into a bird of paradise.

T.T.   *'Perhaps I should have ruffed that heart with my king.'* Timothy the Toucan owes his nickname to a long red nose and a disconcerting habit of bouncing in his chair. Longing for affection, the Toucan tries to ingratiate himself with one and all by admitting every mistake before he makes it. Technically, he is in the same class as R.R. and W.W.

W.W. *'I had twenty I tell you, half the points in the pack.'* Walter the Walrus, a retired accountant since early youth, is an outstanding exponent of the Milton Work Count. Brought up on points and percentages, he espouses in bridge the philosophy of Molière's doctors, firmly believing that it is more honorable to land in the wrong contract with adequate values than to reach the right one without them.

S.B. *'Respect for the Laws is the basis of civilized society.'* The Emeritus Professor of Bio-Sophistry, commonly known as the Secretary Bird, knows the laws backwards and would sooner invoke them against himself than not invoke them at all. Opponents dislike him. Partners fear him. Nobody loves him.

C.C. *'Do you mean that non-vulnerable you would have made fewer tricks?'* Colin the Corgi, a facetious young man from Oxbridge, bites and snaps and rarely troubles to hide his contempt for lesser players. Still lacking in experience, he has all the makings of a future master.

Ch.Ch. *'Thank you Professor, thank you very much.'* Charlie the Chimp is an inveterate chatterbox, interested in every deal except the one he is playing. He likes the inquest on every deal to continue through the next one. This greatly confuses the Rabbit, but then so does everything else.

O.O. *'Curious hand. Both sides can make Four Hearts.'* Oscar the Owl is the most respected figure at the Griffins. The Senior Kibitzer, he is a stern disciplinarian and demands the highest standards in manners and decorum. As Chairman of the Monster Points and Ethics Committees he insists that no partner, not even the Toucan, should be abused or vilified until the deal is over. He frowns on all sharp practice, even when there's no other way to make or break a contract.

P.P. *'A technician is a man who knows exactly what to do the moment he has done something else.'* Peregrine the Penguin is Oscar's opposite number at the Unicorn, where the Griffins play duplicate on Thursdays. Precise and somewhat pompous, the Penguin is a committee man, as well as an accomplished kibitzer, and helps to award Monster Points.

M.M. '*I must make a note of this, a group of men have actually let me have the last word.*' Molly the Mule was the first member of the stronger sex to be admitted to the Griffins. Radiating goodwill to all humankind except the male half, M.M. compensates for her rocky card play with her unshakeability in the post-mortem.

Having met the stars you will know what to expect when you watch them perform.

Books published in the series:

> *Bridge in the Menagerie* (1965)
> *Bridge in the Fourth Dimension* (1974)
> *Masters and Monsters* (1979) Reissued as *Victor Mollo's Bridge Club: How to Turn Masterful Plays into Monstrous Points* (1987)
> *You Need Never Lose at Bridge* (1983)
> *Destiny at Bay* (1987)

After Mollo's death, further books appeared posthumously, some making use of deals and material from previously uncollected articles and others containing new material by Robert and Phillip King, who were assisted by Victor's wife, Squirrel:

> *The Hog in the 21st Century* (by Phillip and Robert King, 1999)
> *Winning Bridge in the Menagerie* (by 'Victor Mollo and Robert King', 2001)
> *Bridge in the Fifth Dimension* (by 'Victor Mollo with P & R King', 2002)
> *Murder in the Menagerie* (by 'Robert King, Phillip King, and Victor Mollo', 2002)

This book is the product of research into Victor Mollo articles that appeared in various periodicals in the 70s and 80s but have never been put together into book form. We discovered some interesting anomalies. The story *Monster Points* appeared in *Master and Monsters*, but the version we include here, whilst having virtually identical text, features different deals. The story *Satan at the Bridge Table* appeared in *Destiny at Bay* under the title *The Prince of Darkness*, but there are significant differences in the early part of the text.

Most exciting of all, we located several 'lost' stories that appear in print here for the first time — they are among the last stories in the book.

ACKNOWLEDGMENTS

This book could not have been brought about without the help of Ron Tacchi, Wolf Klewe, Tim Bourke & Brent Manley.

Mark Horton
Bath, England
November, 2010

1. The Hog Takes to Precision

The Distinguished Stranger, chatting to the Hog in the Griffins' lounge, was drinking water. He appeared to be doing it from choice, so I put him down as an American.

'What shall we play?' he asked the Hog who was to be his partner at our weekly duplicate that night. 'Acol?'

'No, no,' the Hog hastily dismissed the idea. Anyone who pronounced 'Acol' to rhyme with 'able' obviously didn't know the first thing about it.

'Standard American?' suggested the D.S.

'I, er, don't know it very well,' demurred the Hideous Hog. Eyebrows were raised around us. Surely H.H. knew everything very well, or made it up as he went along.

The American tried again. 'Precision?' he ventured. This time the Hog accepted.

'But you don't know Precision,' protested Oscar the Owl, our Senior Kibitzer, after the D.S. had left us.

'True,' agreed the Hog 'but I know Standard American and what better reason could I have for playing Precision?'

'But how will you tell...?' began O.O.

The Hog waved all objections aside. 'No problem. Precision is natural,' he explained. 'Knowing from the start what partner can't have, a good player can work out what he should have. As for the bad player, he can't work anything out anyway, but being simple, Precision is less likely to confuse him than do other systems. So, you see, though I don't know how our friend plays, I am on to a good thing either way.'

After making myself unpopular by winning three rubbers in a row that night, I looked in to see what was happening in the duplicate. As I came up to the Hog's table he was waving the traveling scoresheet and gloating.

'Result merchant,' hissed the Emeritus Professor of Bio-Sophistry, known on account of his habits and appearance as the Secretary Bird. 'Just because he gets a lucky lead he thinks he's done something clever.'

This was the deal they had just played:

Neither Vul.
Dealer North

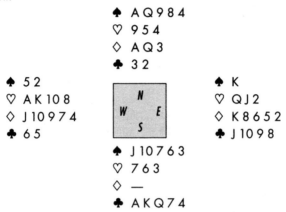

♠ A Q 9 8 4
♡ 9 5 4
◇ A Q 3
♣ 3 2

♠ 5 2
♡ A K 10 8
◇ J 10 9 7 4
♣ 6 5

♠ K
♡ Q J 2
◇ K 8 6 5 2
♣ J 10 9 8

♠ J 10 7 6 3
♡ 7 6 3
◇ —
♣ A K Q 7 4

All the Norths in the room had opened one spade and most Souths responded with two clubs. Some ventured three clubs, but the final contract was everywhere four spades. Deterred by South's bid from starting a club, most Easts led the queen of hearts and thereafter the defense couldn't be denied four tricks, the king of spades scoring by overruffing West's fourth heart.

At the Hog's table the bidding sequence was different:

West	North	East	South
	D.S.		H.H.
	1♠	pass	4◇
pass	4♠	all pass	

Clubs not having been mentioned, the Secretary Bird made the natural lead of the ♣J. Anxious to get rid of his losing hearts and to avoid a club ruff in the process, the D.S. began by laying down the ♠A. When the ♠K dropped he had twelve tricks, an indisputable top.

'Had it only been my lead...,' lamented the Chimp, looking accusingly at S.B.

'Blind chance. No skill at all and we get a bottom,' fumed S.B.

'You don't appreciate the manifold advantages of limit bids,' retorted H.H. scornfully. 'Knowing that partner's high card strength was limited to fifteen and might well be less my first impulse was to go straight to four spades, for a slam seemed most improbable. And yet, if partner had the right cards, a few worthless diamonds, top trumps and the ace of hearts, it might just be on. In our brief discussion about gadgets, partner had told me he was not in favor of playing splinter bids, but four diamonds wasn't likely to be misunderstood. Since it couldn't be a suit, it could only be a cuebid and having the ace himself, partner knew it was a void, so...'

'What has that to do with the Professor's injudicious lead?' broke in the Chimp.

'More than you think' rejoined H.H. 'for whether I bid four spades directly or chanced my arm with what's known, I believe, as an Italian jump cuebid, I had no reason to show my clubs. The other Souths did. Not playing Precision, they had to investigate slam prospects methodically since the opening might be worth eighteen, nineteen or even twenty points.'

'But...' began S.B.

'Of course,' pursued H.H., ignoring him, 'a club might not have been the natural lead. Then it wouldn't have mattered either way. But mark my words: the more you know about partner's hand from the start, the quicker you get to your contract, the less you disclose to opponents on the way, and the greater your chance of a lucky lead. It's a case of heads I win, tails I don't lose, and what could be fairer than that?'

The Hog caressed the traveling scoreslip as he replaced it carefully in its slot. He was beginning to like Precision. He liked it better still after a board he played against Papa the Greek and Karapet the Armenian, the unluckiest player of the current millennium — and before that, too, of course.

The Hideous
Hog

North-South Vul.
Dealer South

```
                        ♠ 9 4 2
                        ♡ A K
                        ◇ K 2
                        ♣ J 10 8 7 5 2
    ♠ K 10 7 5 3
    ♡ J 10 9          ┌──────────┐
    ◇ Q 10 3          │    N     │
    ♣ K 3            W│  W    E  │E
                      │    S     │
                      └──────────┘
```

West	North	East	South
Papa	D.S.	Karapet	H.H.
			1◇
1♠	2♣	pass	2NT
pass	3NT	all pass	

Papa led the ♠5 to Karapet's jack. Playing at top speed, the Hog seized the trick with the ace and crossing to the ♡K called for the ♣J. Karapet followed with the ♣4 and the Hog with the ♣6.

Winning with the king, Papa considered his options. Should he lead a low spade to Karapet's queen, hoping to find him with a third spade? Or should he lay down the king, relying on Karapet to unblock? Surely he couldn't go wrong.

The Greek had already detached the king when a thought suddenly struck him. The Hog had grabbed that first trick very confidently. What if his spade holding was AQx? If he feared a switch wasn't he just the man to win the first trick deceptively with the ace to encourage a continuation?

Looking with new interest at dummy's ◇ K2, Papa conjured up a picture of the Hog's hand. It could be:

♠A Q x   ♡x x x   ◇x x x   ♣A Q x x

Playing Precision, he obviously couldn't open 1♣ and there wasn't quite enough for 1NT. That all-purpose 1◇ would doubtless be his choice and it would explain his play, if, that is, he had ♠AQx and feared a diamond switch. Should either the ♣K or the ◇A be well placed he would have his nine tricks. And if both were wrong his cunning play of the ♠A would allow him to bring off one of his characteristic swindles.

Against Papa? Perish the thought! With a defiant flourish the Greek slapped the ◊3 on the table.

'I'll take my ten tricks' said the Hog, grinning at the kibitzers. This was the complete deal:

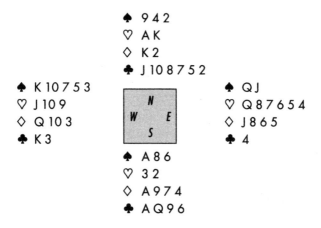

```
              ♠ 9 4 2
              ♡ A K
              ◊ K 2
              ♣ J 10 8 7 5 2
♠ K 10 7 5 3                    ♠ Q J
♡ J 10 9          N            ♡ Q 8 7 6 5 4
◊ Q 10 3      W      E         ◊ J 8 6 5
♣ K 3            S             ♣ 4
              ♠ A 8 6
              ♡ 3 2
              ◊ A 9 7 4
              ♣ A Q 9 6
```

'Just my luck,' sighed Karapet. 'It couldn't happen to anyone else. He has four more cold tricks begging to be cashed and he has to play their suit. Did I tell you what happened to me on...?'

'Yes, you did,' snapped the Hog. Then, with a patronizing look, he addressed Papa. 'I must admit that for once you had a genuine excuse for being clever. I might have held the hand you suspected. That dubious diamond, a feature of Precision, led you astray. It has its snags, of course, though no good player should find them insurmountable. But there's the other side of the picture, the invisible profit it brings. If partner must be careful when he hears one diamond, opponents must be doubly so. It may mean nothing — or something. A bid of convenience — or a genuine suit. And the moment there's a guess to make, there's always the risk of a misguess, as here.

'All in all, I can only claim half the credit,' concluded the Hog modestly. 'My reputation for subtlety accounted for Papa's suspicions. Precision's diamond syndrome did the rest. You should take up Precision, Themistocles, you'll be a new man.'

'Fantastic luck,' spluttered Papa indignantly.

'That's part of the system,' rejoined the Hog with a friendly leer.

Karapet pricked up his ears.

2. Teaching the Rabbit Precision

'The blind leading the blind,' scoffed Oscar the Owl, our Senior Kibitzer at the Griffins. 'You don't know Precision yourself and you have the nerve to teach the Rabbit how to play it.'

'Does it matter what system the Rabbit misplays?' asked Peregrine the Penguin, Oscar's opposite number at the Unicorn.

'Indeed it does,' replied the Hideous Hog. 'Admittedly, if there's a way of misplaying a hand the Rabbit will find it. But the simpler the system, the fewer chances will he have. The charm of Precision,' went on H.H., absent-mindedly picking up the Owl's glass of Bollinger, 'lies in all of the mistakes to which it doesn't lend itself.'

'But you don't know it,' persisted the Owl. 'There must be lots of gadgets and agreements, and variants of this and that, of which you have never heard.'

'That's just it' rejoined H.H. 'I don't have to. If I pined after the Bermuda Bowl or the South Pole Pairs or something equally fatuous, I'd have to learn a set of codes, or rather several sets, ours and theirs, no matter what system I played. But all I want is to win, not honor and glory or a million masterpoints, but hard cash and the odd IMP or two when there's a friendly money match about. And that calls for horse-sense, not science fiction. So give me a simple system which narrows the margin of error. If I know from the start what partner can't have, he won't find it so easy to fool me.'

Scribbling as he spoke, the Hog passed this hand:

♠ J 4 2
♡ 8 4
◇ K Q J 7 6 4
♣ 5 3

'There' he said. 'Neither vulnerable, partner deals and bids one spade. The next man calls four hearts. What do you say?'

'You are playing Precision?' inquired O.O.

'No — every gadget and embellishment in sight but no particular system,' replied H.H. with a grin.

The Penguin pondered. The Owl hooted.

'I pass,' said O.O. 'Partner may have enough to defeat four hearts. And assuming a basic Acol approach, we may have no more than seven spades between us, in which case four spades could cost 800 or even 1100 and all for what may be a phantom sacrifice. This is the right time to be shut out.'

'I concur,' said P.P., 'but what's the catch?'

'I told you a white lie just now,' replied the Hog. 'When this hand came up I was playing Precision with R.R. as my partner. Observe the difference and the simple inferences. He can't have more than fifteen points and may have as few as eleven, so there's no good reason why we should defeat four hearts. I know, also, that we have at least eight spades between us, so I am not haunted by that specter of 800 or 1100. At worst, we'll lose a little on the deal, but against that we may be lucky.'

The Hog jotted down the companion hand:

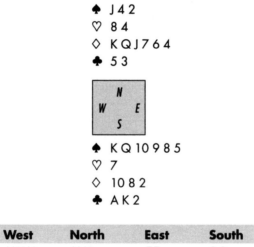

```
        ♠ J 4 2
        ♡ 8 4
        ◇ K Q J 7 6 4
        ♣ 5 3
             N
          W     E
             S
        ♠ K Q 10 9 8 5
        ♡ 7
        ◇ 10 8 2
        ♣ A K 2
```

West	North	East	South
W.W.	H.H.	T.T.	R.R.
			1♠
4♡	4♠	dbl	all pass

'West, that's the Walrus, started with the king of hearts and another to the Toucan's ace. The Rabbit misplayed the hand of course, but the Toucan misdefended, so as usual two wrongs made a right.'

'But what is there to misplay?' asked the Penguin. 'If the first spade doesn't fetch the ace, you ruff a club with the jack and...'

'No, no' broke in the Hog. 'You do no such thing. At trick three you play a diamond, of course. If they are 2-2 it won't matter, but if they are 3-1 you must stake your claim to a singleton before someone else does. Otherwise one of your diamonds will be ruffed.'

The Hog filled in the diagram:

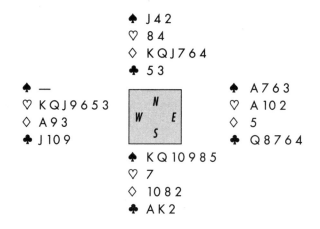

```
              ♠ J 4 2
              ♡ 8 4
              ◇ K Q J 7 6 4
              ♣ 5 3
♠ —                                ♠ A 7 6 3
♡ K Q J 9 6 5 3      N             ♡ A 10 2
◇ A 9 3          W       E         ◇ 5
♣ J 10 9             S             ♣ Q 8 7 6 4
              ♠ K Q 10 9 8 5
              ♡ 7
              ◇ 10 8 2
              ♣ A K 2
```

'Can you imagine the Walrus, or even a sane West for that matter holding up the ace of diamonds or going up with it and promptly leading another? Of course, that Toucan should have overtaken the king of hearts and returned his singleton diamond, playing the Walrus for an ace somewhere. Even as the play went he could have beaten the contract by getting a diamond ruff when he was in with his ace of trumps. A diamond at trick three, driving out the ace, would have scotched that, too, but then no system will solve declarer's play problems. All it can do is to ensure that he hasn't too many to solve.'

The Hog was scribbling again.

Both Vul.
Dealer East

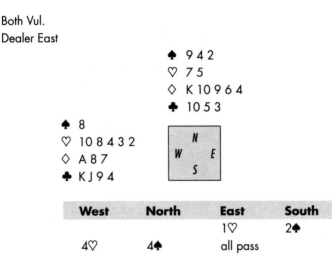

```
                    ♠ 9 4 2
                    ♡ 7 5
                    ◇ K 10 9 6 4
                    ♣ 10 5 3
     ♠ 8
     ♡ 10 8 4 3 2        N
     ◇ A 8 7          W       E
     ♣ K J 9 4            S
```

West	North	East	South
		1♡	2♠
4♡	4♠	all pass	

'You lead the three of hearts to partner's king. The ace of hearts follows. Declarer ruffs, draws two rounds of trumps, dropping partner's queen and continues with the queen of diamonds. Your turn.'

'What does the two spades overcall mean?' inquired P.P. suspiciously.

'Strong' replied the Hog. 'At least six playing tricks, maybe seven and could be eight.'

'So South might or might not have the ace of clubs?' asked the Owl.

'Certainly' said the Hog.

The Owl meditated and slowly shook his head. 'If South has the ace of clubs he began, 'he will make his contract anyway, for unless that queen of diamonds is a singleton he can set up two winners with one ruff. And, needless to say, he can have the jack. Therefore, I go up with the ace of diamonds and lead a low club.'

The Hog chuckled as he filled in the diagram:

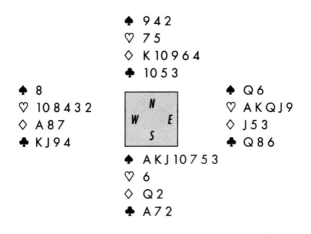

```
                    ♠ 9 4 2
                    ♡ 7 5
                    ◇ K 10 9 6 4
                    ♣ 10 5 3
    ♠ 8                           ♠ Q 6
    ♡ 10 8 4 3 2      N           ♡ A K Q J 9
    ◇ A 8 7       W       E       ◇ J 5 3
    ♣ K J 9 4         S           ♣ Q 8 6
                    ♠ A K J 10 7 5 3
                    ♡ 6
                    ◇ Q 2
                    ♣ A 7 2
```

'You are quite right in assuming that if declarer has the ace of clubs, which is possible, but not certain, he can make his contract,' said H.H., 'but that's only because the queen of diamonds presented you with a problem, so you paused to think and gave the show away. Had you played low smoothly, as if you hadn't a care in the world, declarer wouldn't have known what to do. Should he play you for the ace or finesse against the jack? Should he...'

'What has all this to do with Precision?' broke in the Penguin testily.

'Everything,' replied the Hog, 'for I happened to be playing Precision, again with none other than the Rabbit as my partner. You had a problem when declarer led the queen of diamonds for you couldn't tell who had the ace of clubs. I had no problem for I knew that the Rabbit couldn't have it. He had concealed the queen and jack of hearts from declarer, good play, so it was doubtless accidental, but he couldn't conceal them from me, so I could count twelve points in his hand, ten in hearts and two in spades. Another ace and he would have opened one club. My only chance, then, was to find the cards as they were and to hope that declarer would take the wrong view.

'Knowing what partner can't have helps in defense, as well as in the bidding,' declared the Hog. 'I had to put declarer to a guess, for it was that or nothing, and anyone can misguess, you know,' added H.H., casting down his eyes modestly. 'Even I... in January...'

3. Precision and the Money Motif

'Ridiculous!' said Oscar the Owl, our Senior Kibitzer at the Griffins.

'Absurd!' echoed Peregrine the Penguin, his opposite number at the Unicorn.

'What is?' I inquired.

The Hog, they explained, was no longer content to practice Precision with the Rabbit at duplicate, he was now playing it with him for money.

We were sipping a pre-prandial Madeira at the Griffins Bar and before long H.H. himself came up to join us.

'Is it true,' I asked him, 'that you are now playing it with him for money? What's the idea?'

'I'm a result merchant,' replied the Hog simply. 'I have no interest in cups and trophies and all those platonic things that are their own reward, for Heaven knows they bring no other. I play to win money, while most of my partners, alas, play to lose it. Precision helps me to get the better of them, to save them from themselves, so to speak. Yes, it's a system ideal for rubber bridge, where partner is so often the most dangerous of the three opponents at the table.'

'But how can you stop the Rabbit, or the Walrus or the Toucan, for that matter, from fooling you, whatever system they play?' objected O.O.

'Of course you can't,' agreed the Hog, 'but that's where Precision scores, don't you see. The bids and responses being strictly limited, the margin of deception isn't nearly so wide. Why the Rabbit himself will do well to fool you by more than a point or two. Even he, you know, can count up to sixteen — well, when he's in form anyway. And even the Rabbit can usually tell a five-card suit when he sees one. So from the start, before he has a chance to mislead you, you can have a pretty good idea of what's going to happen.'

From his capacious pockets the Hog produced a long, crumpled envelope and hastily scribbled on the back:

♠ 4
♡ J 7 6 5 3
◇ 8 5
♣ Q J 9 5 3

'Your partner opens one heart and the next man calls one spade. Your turn, Oscar'

'Precision?' inquired the Owl.

'No,' replied the Hog. 'That's just the point.'

The Owl blinked, but the Hog wouldn't take that for an answer.

'Four hearts,' he hazarded at last.

'Not much else you can say' agreed P.P. 'Silly hand.'

'There's a catch somewhere,' I said.

'The catch, if you bid four hearts, will come on the next round,' replied H.H., 'for opponents will surely call four spades. What will you do then? Leave in partner's double? Pass or bid five hearts, if you have to speak first? Partner being virtually unlimited, you can't be sure to whom the hand belongs or who is doing the sacrificing.'

'Sacrificing!' repeated P.P. in shocked tones. 'Aren't you always telling us, H.H., that just as a good soldier is not the one who dies for his country, but the one who makes the enemy die for his, so the only good sacrifice is by opponents, when you can't make your own contract anyway?'

'Quite right,' declared the Hog. 'At rubber bridge or IMPs the dice are heavily loaded against sacrificing. If you go down 500 five times to save 600 and then do it once too often, when they would have gone down themselves, you end up losing. So it's not enough to be right five times out of six.'

'Then I pass four spades,' said O.O., 'for I certainly can't be sure that once in six times partner won't have enough to beat it. I don't like passing, but I like phantoms even less.'

'And now' resumed H.H., 'suppose that you are playing Precision, as I was when this hand came up. The moment I heard one heart, I was virtually certain that opponents could make four spades. Firstly, partner had a five or six-card suit, so come what may we couldn't make more than one trick in hearts. Secondly, his maximum was fifteen points, leaving eleven apart from the hypothetical ace of hearts. So, to give us any chance, every point in his hand had to be working full time, and that, as you know, rarely happens. No longer could partner have eighteen or nineteen points or four hearts to the ace king, which might be worth two tricks in defense. Playing Precision, there were no phantoms to haunt me.'

'You knew your fate' conceded O.O., 'but how did it help you to avert it? What did you do?'

'Over one spade I bid two diamonds,' said H.H.

'The system bid, of course,' remarked P.P.

'System my foot!' snapped the Hog. 'The system told me where my opponents would get to, not how to stop them getting there. That was up to me. Since my objective was to be doubled, I tried to make the penalty seem attractive, to induce each defender in turn to over-estimate the value of his diamond honors; in short, to confuse the issue at no cost to our side, since I was prepared to play five hearts from the start. Partner turned up with:

♠752   ♡KQ10986   ◇A43   ♣A

We were certainly lucky to make the contract, but even one down, or two down for that matter, would have been a good result, for we couldn't have stopped five spades. From the word *Go*, I had a preview of the finale.'

As he spoke, the Hog was jotting down another hand.

'There,' he said. 'You are playing Precision with the Rabbit, who opens two clubs. You bid two diamonds, asking him for further information, and hear three clubs. In case you don't know, that means a six-card suit and a trick outside. What's your destination?'

We studied the Hog's hand:

♠ Q752
♡ AQ
◇ AK
♣ Q10532

'I'll settle for six clubs,' ventured O.O.

'With the Rabbit in charge, five clubs is enough,' I said cautiously. 'He's sure to find some way of losing a trick in the play.'

'If partner has a club suit,' observed Peregrine the Penguin 'you'd get to five or six clubs in any system.'

'Exactly,' agreed the Hog, 'but are you sure that it's where you want to get to?'

Nobody said anything and H.H. went on. 'You could have two spades to lose, you know. I couldn't because the three clubs rebid showed specifically a trick outside clubs. Incidentally he needn't have had six clubs. The two clubs bid might have been based on five good clubs and a four-card major, in which case the slam would depend on the quality of the major.'

'Couldn't you have found out? Can you find out about the spade holding now?' asked the Owl.

'Certainly' replied the Hog. 'All the machinery is there, and with a different partner I might have used it — especially,' he added as an afterthought, 'if I were more familiar with it myself.' That's the beauty of Precision. On the same hand you can be savant and scientific or daring and direct, suiting your style to the occasion, and above all, to your partner.'

'There was, of course, a small precaution to take,' went on H.H. 'I had to ensure that the hand should be played from the right side of the table.'

'The ace-queen of hearts...' began the Penguin.

'That too,' replied the Hog. 'The lead can be important, but it's more important still that the right player should be dummy, where he can do no harm. Besides, if we could make six clubs we should also make six notrump, which proved to be an excellent contract. But judge for yourselves.'

```
              ♠ A J 4
              ♡ 10 5
              ◇ 9 7
              ♣ A K J 9 8 4
              ┌─────────┐
              │    N    │
              │ W     E │
              │    S    │
              └─────────┘
              ♠ Q 7 5 2
              ♡ A Q
              ◇ A K
              ♣ Q 10 5 3 2
```

Lead: ◇Q

'Just about a fifty-fifty chance,' observed the Owl. 'What's so wonderful about that?'

'A three-three break or a finesse or an endplay. I make it roughly three to one in my favor,' rejoined the Hog.

'But if you try the spades and run up against the likely 4-2 break, you can lose two tricks and it will be too late then for the heart finesse,' countered O.O.

'You can't eat your cake and have it,' said P.P. sagely.

'Of course you can,' retorted the Hog 'and that's always been my system. I ran a few clubs, just for fun to see if anyone squirmed, and continued with the ace and four of spades. Had East gone up with the king, it would have been all over. West won, however, and returned another diamond, giving me time to test the suit before falling back on the heart finesse.'

With that the Hog screwed up the crumpled envelope and was about to throw it away when Oscar stopped him.

'Careful!' he warned, 'there's a letter inside.'

'No, no,' the Hog was quick to reassure him. 'It is a greeting card for R.R.'s sister, Rowena, but her birthday was over a fortnight ago, so it's no use now. I promised the Rabbit to post it and left it in this suit. It's been much too cold to wear it lately. Wretched weather...'

Papa the Greek

4. The Play Is in the Bidding

Nibbling caviar canapés over a magnum of Bollinger, we sat discussing the match in the Griffins Bar.

'Result merchant!' scoffed Oscar the Owl, our senior kibitzer. 'You're enthusiastic about Precision all because you've had some good results playing it with the Rabbit. What does that prove?'

'Any system that makes for good results with the Rabbit must have merit,' replied the Hog.

Peregrine the Penguin, O.O.'s opposite number at the Unicorn, shook his head gravely. 'I'd be more impressed by a system that yielded good results with Garozzo,' he said.

'Wrong as usual,' said H.H. 'Amazing how consistent you are, Peregrine. Garozzo will get good results playing any system, though he, too, incidentally, plays Precision.'

'Super Precision,' corrected P.P.

'Certainly,' agreed the Hog, 'and if he played Acol, it would be Super Acol.'

'And Super Standard American?' suggested the Owl with a malicious twinkle in his eye.

'No.' The Hog brushed that aside firmly. 'Standard American isn't so much a system as a collection of taboos. It was fine in Culbertson's day, but rigor mortis set in long ago and not even Garozzo could transform it into Super Rigor Mortis. Anyway,' went on H.H., warming to his subject, 'all top pairs use a subtle bidding language of their own, a super language, if you like. The system provides no more than a broad framework.'

'Are you saying,' asked the Penguin sceptically, 'that you use with the Rabbit the same framework as Garozzo did with Belladonna or Eric Rodwell does with Jeff Meckstroth or Larry Cohen did with....'

'Exactly the same,' the Hog assured him. 'You look disbelieving because you confuse the system with the frills and titbits, the treatments and the gadgets that can be grafted on to it. A strong camel can carry a heavy load and if your system is basically simple and flexible you can do almost anything with it — or nothing, keeping it simple throughout as I do with the Rabbit. You saw that this afternoon, didn't you?'

The annual match between the Bacchanalians and the Pterodactyls had been for the most part, a tame affair with a succession of flat hands. Two swings proved decisive and in both systemic considerations played a part.

This was the eighth board. I watched Papa play the hand before taking the set to the other room.

Neither Vul.
Dealer South

```
                    ♠ 5 3 2
                    ♡ Q 7 5
                    ◇ K Q J 10
                    ♣ 7 6 5
   ♠ K J 9 6                          ♠ A Q 10
   ♡ 10 9 8         ┌──────────┐      ♡ J
   ◇ A 5 4 3        │    N     │      ◇ 9 8 6 2
   ♣ 10 4        W  │          │  E   ♣ J 9 8 3 2
                    │    S     │
                    └──────────┘
                    ♠ 8 7 4
                    ♡ A K 6 4 3 2
                    ◇ 7
                    ♣ A K Q
```

West	North	East	South
Ch.Ch.	Karapet	C.C.	Papa
			1♡
pass	2♡	pass	3♣
pass	3◇	pass	4♡
all pass			

The Hog and the Rabbit also reached 4♡, though by a different route, and both declarers adopted the same line of play. Each time the lead was the ♡10. On the second round of trumps East threw a low diamond. The average Life Master would have now played a diamond, while the ♡Q was still in dummy as an entry. Not so Papa and the Hog, who drew the last trump before touching diamonds.

Charlie the Chimp, sitting West for the Bacchanalians, went up with the ◇A and promptly switched to a spade.

'Flat board,' observed Papa conceding defeat. 'You can neither stop short of game nor make it.'

Defending against the Hideous Hog, Molly the Mule held up the ◊A, waiting for her partner, Walter the Walrus, to give her a count. Thereupon the Hog spread his hand and claimed.

'That was surely a piece of luck which might have gone the other way,' commented O.O., stirring the ice in the bucket.

'It was nothing of the sort,' retorted the Hog. 'The play, of course, was elementary. Dummy's only entry must be removed first, otherwise West has nothing to gain by holding up the ace of diamonds. Call it a Reverse Merrimac. You gain access to dummy by killing its entry and...'

'But Papa did all that,' broke in the Owl.

'A waste of time after that tell-tale bidding sequence,' rejoined the Hog. 'Papa's opening one heart being virtually unlimited, he had to catch up. After all, had he found Karapet with the ace of spades instead of wasted valued in diamonds, there might have been a slam about. Hence three clubs. But then, over three diamonds, he neither tries three notrump nor cuebids spades. With so clear a picture before him the Chimp had no reason to hold up the ace of diamonds. Unless Colin the Corgi had the ace of spades there was no hope. He couldn't go wrong. Compare that with our Precision sequence:

H.H.	R.R.
1♣	1NT
2♡	3♡
4♡	pass

I didn't have to investigate. Unlike Papa who had so much more than he might have, I had told partner that I was good and he had told me what he had, or rather hadn't. The less revealing the sequence, the more difficult it is to defend against it. So much for luck.'

ANOTHER FLAT BOARD

At half time, when Papa and Karapet came over to face the Hog and the Rabbit, the Bacchanalians had a slender lead of 220 total points. I watched the play from a seat between Papa and the Rabbit. Again the hands were uneventful and when the last board was placed on the table I thought it might well decide the match.

Both Vul.
Dealer South

```
                    ♠ 7
                    ♡ K J 9 7 6 5
                    ◇ 6 3
                    ♣ 9 8 6 5
        ♠ Q J 8 2
        ♡ 2                 ┌─────────┐
        ◇ A Q J 8          │    N    │
        ♣ A Q 7 3          │ W     E │
                           │    S    │
                           └─────────┘
```

West	North	East	South
Papa	*R.R.*	*Karapet*	*H.H.*
			1♣
pass	2♡	pass	3NT
dbl	pass	pass	redbl
all pass			

'Does two hearts mean a six-card suit and four to seven points?' enquired Karapet.

The Hog nodded in the affirmative, noting with relief that the Rabbit didn't blush or gurgle. Evidently he had remembered the system.

Papa's double was too casual, too lackadaisical to conceal the joy he felt in his heart. Here at last was the hand to win the match. His singleton heart presaged a bad break in dummy's long, broken suit, and where else could H.H. look for tricks?

The Hog's redouble was a formality, a courtesy to partner, good for morale and disturbing to opponents. Besides he expected to make the contract.

In anticipation of a pleasurable holocaust, Papa led the ♣3. Karapet played the ♣10 and the Hog won with the ♣K! The ♡A, ♡Q and ♡3 followed in quick succession. So the long suit sprang no leaks — a bitter blow to Papa who had to find five tiresome discards. The ♠A and ◇K would bring the Hog's points up to the required 16, but that would only come to eight tricks. Karapet was marked with the ♣J, since it had taken the ♣K to capture the ♣10, and it was to be hoped that he had the ♠K. Otherwise H.H. would have nine tricks. So Papa boldly shed his ♣A and ♣Q, retaining the ♣7 to put Karapet in for a diamond lead through the closed hand. When the Hog called for dummy's last heart Papa remained with:

```
          ♠ Q J 8
          ♡ —
          ◊ A Q J
          ♣ 7
```

The Hog, who had discarded the ◊2 and the ♣4, now threw the ◊K. Papa thereupon parted with the ♣7. Their eyes met as, with a leer which was doubtless intended as a smile, the Hog led a club from dummy and produced the one card he surely couldn't have, the ♣J.

'Having no, I mean, having a...' began the Rabbit. Then his voice faded away.

The Greek paused to regroup. If the Hog had the ♠A he would have nine tricks and the Bacchanalians would surely win the match. But since H.H. had the ♣J he could have 16 points with the ♠K and not the ♠A and that would still come to no more than eight tricks, provided that Papa kept his nerve. So he threw a spade. With a loud guffaw, H.H. claimed the rest.

This was the deal in full:

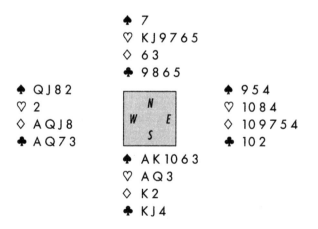

```
                    ♠ 7
                    ♡ K J 9 7 6 5
                    ◊ 6 3
                    ♣ 9 8 6 5
    ♠ Q J 8 2          N          ♠ 9 5 4
    ♡ 2           W         E     ♡ 10 8 4
    ◊ A Q J 8          S          ◊ 10 9 7 5 4
    ♣ A Q 7 3                     ♣ 10 2
                    ♠ A K 10 6 3
                    ♡ A Q 3
                    ◊ K 2
                    ♣ K J 4
```

'Another flat board I expect,' gloated the Hog.

'Played in one spade making nine tricks,' said Oscar, who had watched the board already in the other room. 'Hardly surprising. Once South decides not to open two notrump, West's singleton heart rules out a double and North is only too glad to pass.'

The Hog was still chuckling when Molly the Mule and Walter the Walrus, who thought that they had just won, came in from the other room.

'Do you make it 2600 or have I left something out?' purred the Hog.

'Did you have to double a cold, cast-iron game contract?' asked Molly, fixing Papa with a steely gaze.

'Yes,' replied Papa defiantly. 'Since you didn't trouble to bid the cold, cast iron game, they would have won anyway, unless I doubled and got them down.'

'I suppose we should be thankful that they didn't bid a grand slam,' said Molly, 'but no matter what happens, of course, a man must have the last word.'

Thereupon she sailed out of the room.

5. When in Doubt, Play Precision

'Precision's not for me,' said Karapet sadly. 'It's geared to get the best out of good cards, but what if you don't get them? Does it matter whether I need sixteen points or seventeen to open one club if my average holding is six or seven?'

The subject came up during a discussion on the eve of the annual match between the Pterodactyls and the Salamanders. Colin the Corgi was to have as his partner an overseas member, who had been playing with us for some days. Nobody could remember his name, typically Australian — something like Robinson or Taylor or Gewartzberger — but he had large, flat, outwardly oriented feet and a distinctly unbalanced shape, so he soon came to be known as the Platypus. Since it was fashionable in London, he was ready to play Acol. He didn't like it, but then he didn't know it, so perhaps he was doing it an injustice. Colin countered with offers of Standard American, the Polish Club or 2/1. Disliking all in equal measure, he had no bias and any one of the three would do.

'Why not play Precision?' suggested the Hog.

'I don't know it terribly well,' objected the Platypus.

'Neither do I,' echoed the Corgi.

'Then,' pursued H.H., 'whatever system you adopt, neither of you will ever be sure what the other has, but at least, playing Precision, you will know what he hasn't and that's a great help, you know. So much less can go wrong, and so long as you keep out of trouble I, er, that is, we will bring in the points.'

The Salamanders, led by Papa the Greek and Karapet the Armenian, the unluckiest player in recent times, and before that, too, of course, faced the Hog and the Rabbit.

The Pterodactyls made a poor start. An unlucky defense by the Rabbit, who placed declarer with the fourteenth diamond, which he didn't have, allowed the Salamanders to make a slam that failed in the other room. On the next deal the Hog had the better of the auction, outbidding the Rabbit to bring in a difficult game in spades. In notrump, the Rabbit might well have found the losing line of play. Then came this deal:

Both Vul.
Dealer South

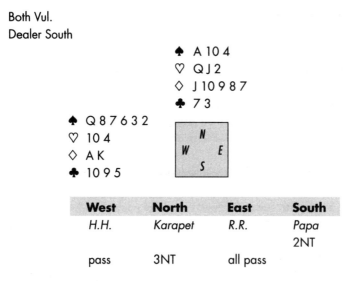

♠ A 10 4
♡ Q J 2
◇ J 10 9 8 7
♣ 7 3

♠ Q 8 7 6 3 2
♡ 10 4
◇ A K
♣ 10 9 5

West	North	East	South
H.H.	Karapet	R.R.	Papa
			2NT
pass	3NT	all pass	

The Hog started with the ♠2. On that bidding, he told us later, a true card could only help declarer, while partner, who couldn't have anything, anyway, mattered less than ever.

Papa played low from dummy and won the Rabbit's nine with the king. At trick two he led a low diamond and the Hog was in with the ◇A. Sitting between H.H. and dummy, I could see no possible defence.

Whatever Papa made of the lead, he would insert dummy's ten on the spade continuation and lose the trick to the Rabbit's ♠J, with which he was marked by the play at trick one. Since Papa wouldn't have opened 2NT with a singleton ♠K, however, the Rabbit couldn't have a third spade, so whatever he returned, the Greek would have time to clear the diamonds before the Hog could set up his spades. The only consolation for the Pterodactyls supporters was that the result would doubtless be the same in the other room.

I had just reached this conclusion when the Hog calmly produced the ♠Q. Of course Papa assumed that the ♠J was behind the ♠Q and allowed the ♠Q to hold, hoping that East had only three spades and the ◇K. A third spade cleared the suit and the diamond king was still intact. The Hog had stolen a tempo and the contract with it.

```
                    ♠ A 10 4
                    ♡ Q J 2
                    ◇ J 10 9 8 7
                    ♣ 7 3
   ♠ Q 8 7 6 3 2                        ♠ J 9
   ♡ 10 4              N                ♡ 9 8 7 5 3
   ◇ A K           W       E            ◇ 4
   ♣ 10 9 5              S              ♣ Q 8 6 4 2
                    ♠ K 5
                    ♡ A K 6
                    ◇ Q 6 5 3 2
                    ♣ A K J
```

'Oh what a clever ruse!' exclaimed an enthusiastic kibitzer.

Papa turned on him in a flash.

'Clever?' he repeated scornfully. 'A clever imitation, perhaps, but let me tell you that I found this defense years ago when I was on safari in Kenya. No doubt the Hog read about it in Barry Rigal's book and now claims it as his own. I fully expect,' went on Papa, rather less confidently 'that our West in the other room will execute the same routine stratagem. Stands out a mile.'

The Hog shook his head. 'Your West won't get the chance, my dear Themistocles. Our other pair is playing Precision, you know,' explained the Hog in the patronizing tone which never failed to infuriate Papa.

'I suppose that they won't get to game,' jeered the Greek.

'On the contrary' retorted H.H.,' not only will they get to game, but they'll find the right one too. In Precision your hand, Papa, doesn't qualify for two notrump — the system bid is one club, which allows the extra bidding space to bring to light the 5-5 diamond fit. On my hand, your West will bid one spade over which North, lacking the values for a free bid of one notrump, will surely call two diamonds.

'A splendid start,' broke in the enthusiastic kibitzer, 'but with such unfortunate duplication isn't there now a grave risk of ending in six diamonds?'

'None,' the Hog assured him. 'Over two diamonds South calls three diamonds, a trump asking bid, and North bids three hearts, a one step response denying any of the three top honors. No question of a slam after that, and the contract will be five diamonds.

'With no room to maneuver,' went on H.H., 'Karapet had to bid three notrump. The one club opening provides the space to bring to light both the fit in diamonds and the weakness in top trumps. Next time Papa goes big game hunting,' concluded the Hog with a friendly leer at the kibitzers, 'he will learn that on good hands it pays to keep the bidding low. An outstanding card holder, such as he, would lose a lot less at rubber bridge, playing Precision.'

6. The Case Against Precision

The Hideous Hog and Oscar the Owl, our Senior Kibitzer, were alone at the Griffins Bar. The Owl was saying, 'You've had some pretty good results at duplicate playing Precision with the Rabbit, H.H. Have you considered popularizing it at rubber bridge? It might do something to raise the level of the game here.'

'Then why should I popularize it?' retorted the Hog. 'Or do you take me for some crazy philanthropist, like those guilt-conscious millionaires who try to expiate past sins with donations to worthy causes? I've no sins to expiate.'

'But surely,' persisted O.O., 'you prefer good bridge to bad bridge.'

'Certainly,' agreed H.H. '*Ars gratia artis.* I am all in favor of high class bridge, providing that it's not at my expense. I don't mind a bit if my opponents play well so long as they don't stop playing badly.'

'But that's a contradiction in terms,' protested the Owl.

'A superficial view,' replied the Hog. 'What is good play? Ask any expert. It's executing smother plays and criss-cross squeezes, reaching delicate slams on combined 22-counts and finding brilliant sacrifices at the seven-level. Very enjoyable and good copy for the columnists, but how often does it happen? Not often enough to affect materially my balance sheet at the end of the year. That's why I'm not worried by good play, not in the accepted sense of the word. There's not enough scope for it. What I can't afford is to miss out on those frequent and lucrative errors which spring from not knowing whether the hand belongs to our side or theirs, whether partner's opening is weak or strong, whether his suit is long or short. It's because Precision runs counter to nature's laws of confusion that I don't want to see it take on at the Griffins.'

The Hog beckoned to the barman. 'This gentleman, I think, would like to order another bottle, Curlew. Where was I? Oh yes, confusion. Minor-suit three-bids are a perfect example. What does it signify when partner opens three clubs or three diamonds?'

'I...' began the Owl.

Raising imperiously a pink, fat forefinger, the Hog stopped him. 'Wrong, Oscar. Whatever you were going to say you would have been wrong, for the riddle is insoluble. I've seen the most respectable people open three diamonds on seven to the jack and not a rag outside, and also on a suit headed by the ace, queen, jack with a queen in the offing. It all depends on the individual, his styles, his mood — what happened on the previous hand, maybe. Where the margin between minimum and maximum is so wide, there are endless opportunities for turmoil and trouble, and, therefore, for the most promising and expensive misunderstandings. Precision,' pursued H.H., 'not only narrows that profit margin, but often eliminates it altogether. The system won't make poor players bid well, but time and again it will stop them from bidding badly, which is manifestly unfair to their opponents. Let me show you two deals to bring the point home.'

'Precision?' asked the Owl.

'Only the second one,' replied H.H. 'The first came up here at the Griffins, the other day.'

Neither Vul.
Dealer East

```
                    ♠ J 10 9 8 7
                    ♡ A K
                    ◇ —
                    ♣ A J 9 7 6 5
  ♠ Q 5 4 2              N          ♠ —
  ♡ 7 5 3                           ♡ 10 9 8 6 4 2
  ◇ A Q 7 6 2       W        E      ◇ 4
  ♣ 2                     S         ♣ K Q 10 8 4 3
                    ♠ A K 6 3
                    ♡ Q J
                    ◇ K J 10 9 8 5 3
                    ♣ —
```

West	North	East	South
M.M.	R.R.	C.C.	H.H.
		3♣	dbl
pass	pass	3♡	4◇
pass	4♡	pass	5◇
pass	5♡	pass	5♠
pass	6♠	pass	pass
dbl	all pass		

'North's bidding seems a little exotic,' observed the Owl.

'Unorthodox,' corrected the Hog. 'The Rabbit made the addition and his hand came to eighteen. He counted thirteen in top cards, four for the void in diamonds, one for the doubleton heart and two more for the long clubs.'

'But that's twenty,' objected O.O.

'Less two points as a safety margin to allow for errors in accountancy,' explained the Hog. 'Having been done out of a luscious penalty, the Rabbit wasn't prepared to settle for anything less than a slam — in spades, needless to say. Despite my tiresome preoccupation with diamonds, the original double guaranteed reputable spades, but he had to maneuver me into the driving seat. Apart from bidding, cardplay is the weakest part of his game, so he had to make sure that the hand was played from the right side.'

'Communications are going to present a problem,' observed O.O., after studying the deal closely.

'True,' agreed the Hog. 'Fortunately, I could place every pip. The original three-bid located the high cards, while the rescue into hearts gave me a complete picture of the distribution.'

'What happened?' asked O.O.

'Molly led her singleton club. Needing three entries to set up and enjoy the diamonds,' pursued the Hog, 'I ruffed in hand and led the king of diamonds, covered and ruffed in dummy. Coming back with the king of trumps, I continued with the jack of diamonds again covered and ruffed. Returning with a trump to the ace, I led out my diamond winners discarding dummy's ace and king of hearts to unblock, then a club. When I came to my sixth diamond this was the five-card ending:

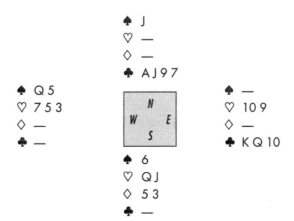

If Molly ruffed low I would overruff in dummy and ruff a club. Molly, of course, could overruff but she would then have to put me in hand with a heart. So she ruffed the diamond with the queen of spades, intending to return a trump and so lock me in dummy — if I let her.'

The Owl blinked.

'Quite right,' said the Hog. 'I jettisoned dummy's jack of spades under the queen and now it didn't matter whether Molly returned a heart or the five of spades. Either way I would be in my hand with three winners to cash.'

'Molly must have been pleased!' said the Owl.

'For once,' chortled H.H., 'she could not think of anything sarcastic to say to her partner. Since the anarchic three-bid promises nothing, she couldn't reproach him for turning up with a minus quantity. She blamed me instead for having the six of spades in place of the five. 'I suppose,' she told the Rabbit, 'you took that into account when you bid that ridiculous slam."

The Owl hooted.

'That one deal was worth nearly a case of Bollinger, even at today's prices. And you want me to popularize Precision — and go on the water wagon, I suppose!'

Another deal was before us.

'There,' said the Hog. 'This time we are playing Precision. It's duplicate at the Unicorn and I have a good partner, Colin the Corgi, and strong opponents too, Papa and Karapet. With neither side vulnerable, the Corgi opens three clubs, which Papa doubles. You hold:

$$\spadesuit \quad J\,3\,2$$
$$\heartsuit \quad A\,K\,J\,6$$
$$\diamondsuit \quad A\,K\,J\,10$$
$$\clubsuit \quad Q\,3$$

'If I am not mistaken,' ventured O.O., 'the three-bid guarantees a seven-card suit with two of the three top honors and an ace or king outside.'

'Which can only be in spades,' rejoined the Hog. 'If it's the ace, we have twelve top tricks. If it's the king, we may need a finesse or squeeze, and after Papa's double it must be an odds-on chance. So I bid six clubs. No great problem.'

'Presumably he made it.' said the Owl.

'He certainly would have done,' agreed H.H. 'but Papa had no intention of going quietly. He calmly bid six hearts, expecting to go four down. At matchpoint scoring, 800 against 920 would have been worthwhile.'

'And is that what it was, 800?' inquired O.O.

'Or thereabouts,' replied H.H., 'but as I told you, I had a good partner, so I declined the penalty, preferring to play in six notrump.'

"But the lead...' began the Owl.

'No, no,' the Hog quickly stopped him. 'Of course the lead had to run up to him.'

'But how?' The Owl was sorely puzzled.

'Simple. I bid six spades!' explained the Hog, filling in the other hands.

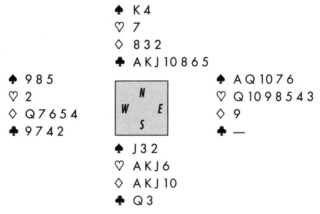

```
                    ♠ K 4
                    ♡ 7
                    ◊ 8 3 2
                    ♣ A K J 10 8 6 5
    ♠ 9 8 5                              ♠ A Q 10 7 6
    ♡ 2                     N            ♡ Q 10 9 8 5 4 3
    ◊ Q 7 6 5 4        W         E       ◊ 9
    ♣ 9 7 4 2              S             ♣ —
                    ♠ J 3 2
                    ♡ A K J 6
                    ◊ A K J 10
                    ♣ Q 3
```

'I suppose,' hazarded the Owl doubtfully, 'that it couldn't be a genuine suit.'

'Impossible' declared the Hog. 'Playing Precision, a good major is shown on the first round. It is the routine response and since I hadn't made it, I could not have suddenly discovered a good spade suit, fit to bid at the six-level. Colin got the message and promptly converted to six notrump. And this time Papa had to subside. At no form of scoring would it pay to go down 1100.

'You see the difference,' concluded the Hog, looking wistfully at the empty bottle. 'On the first deal, Molly couldn't be sure of a single high card in her partner's hand, whereas I could play double dummy. This time, hearing the disciplined Precision opening, I could place every card that mattered, and accordingly bid double dummy. So let's hear no more about popularizing Precision at the Griffins, Oscar. The recession must get along without me.'

7. Precision in the Menagerie

We were dining at the Griffins after an eventful session.

'I'm not like Karapet,' declared Molly the Mule, passing the port the wrong way. 'Self-pity is essentially a masculine trait. To pretend one holds worse cards than anyone else is nonsense, superstition, masochism. What does happen though, and I've noticed it time and again, is that some people seem fated to run into bad breaks more often than others do, and some people,' went on Molly, fixing Timothy the Toucan with a steely eye, 'invariably cut the worst player at the table and find him at his deadliest. What's the answer to that?'

'Try playing Precision,' advised the Hog, peeling a walnut.

'What good will that do when partner is imbued with the death wish?' asked M.M.

'You can put the weapons of self-destruction out of his reach,' replied H.H. 'Remove the razor, the weedkiller, the knotted cord. Think what Precision has done for the Rabbit. One squeak from him and I know whether he has a hand that's balanced or distributional, below or above the 16 points dividing line. Playing in the usual way, he doesn't know it himself until the third or fourth round of bidding when it's too late. Playing Precision, confusing partner isn't nearly so easy.'

'Nuts!' was Molly's only comment. The Hog noted how flushed she looked. After the Hermitage '75 and the Richebourg '69, the moment seemed ripe for a sporting challenge.

'You've established close rapport with Charlie the Chimp, a fine gifted player,' he began. 'How would it be if the Rabbit and I took you on, playing Precision? The usual stakes with a modest side-bet of, say, a case of Bollinger per rubber?'

'Done,' said Molly.

And so an unfriendly match was arranged. I missed the beginning, but soon after I sat down to kibitz this hand come along:

Neither Vul.
Dealer South

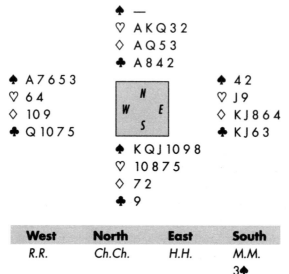

```
                    ♠ —
                    ♡ A K Q 3 2
                    ◇ A Q 5 3
                    ♣ A 8 4 2
    ♠ A 7 6 5 3                      ♠ 4 2
    ♡ 6 4            N                ♡ J 9
    ◇ 10 9       W       E           ◇ K J 8 6 4
    ♣ Q 10 7 5       S               ♣ K J 6 3
                    ♠ K Q J 10 9 8
                    ♡ 10 8 7 5
                    ◇ 7 2
                    ♣ 9
```

West	North	East	South
R.R.	Ch.Ch.	H.H.	M.M.
			3♠
pass	4♠	all pass	

The Owl and two lesser kibitzers complimented the Chimp on his bold, imaginative raise on a void.

The Rabbit led the ◇10. Molly went up with dummy's ◇A, cashed the ♣A and, to get to her hand, ruffed a club. The Rabbit won the next trick with the ♠A and returned the ◇9, then a club. Forced a second time, Molly lost trump control and the hand collapsed.

'Now you see what I mean by bad breaks,' she fumed, turning to the Hog. 'I could stand finding a void opposite, or a 5-2 trump break, but not both. That would be too much for anyone.'

The Hog's leer was distinctly unsympathetic.

'I suppose none of it would have happened had we been playing Precision.' scoffed Molly.

'True,' agreed the Hog. 'Not that it would have mattered for game or slam would still be there.'

'At the Butterflies,' rejoined Molly with spirit, 'jeering when opponents have had an unlucky hand is considered bad form, but we are only a ladies' club, of course.'

It was time for O.O. to intervene.

'H.H. has at times an unfortunate way of putting things,' he began, 'but I am sure that he didn't intend to be sarcastic. He was doubtless trying to point out that playing Precision a three-bid guarantees a seven-card suit, so you can't run into a 5-2 break, which, incidentally, isn't as rare as all that. The 4-3 split is, you know, only a sixty-two percent chance.'

'Does there have to be a void opposite?' cried Molly growing increasingly exasperated.

'Of course not,' agreed the Owl, 'but then in Precision a three-bid excludes a four-card side suit, especially a major, so you wouldn't be playing in spades anyway. And you will note that it only requires a 2-2 break to make six hearts a certainty.'

'As the cards are,' chipped in the Hog, 'a grand slam in hearts is unbeatable. Mind you,' he added modestly, 'I don't say that we would have got there, not every time anyway.'

Precision came to the fore again a few hands later. Since H.H. became declarer he is shown, for the sake of convenience, as South.

Both Vul.
Dealer South

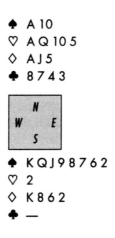

♠ A 10
♡ A Q 10 5
◇ A J 5
♣ 8 7 4 3

♠ K Q J 9 8 7 6 2
♡ 2
◇ K 8 6 2
♣ —

West	North	East	South
M.M.	R.R.	Ch.Ch.	H.H.
			4♠
pass	5♣	dbl	5♠
pass	6♠	all pass	

Before Molly made the opening lead the Hog informed her that R.R.'s 5♣ was a Control Asking Bid. 'And H.H. told me that he had the ace,' explained the Rabbit.

The Chimp shot up in his chair.

'Or it could be a void,' R.R. corrected himself hastily. 'With a singleton club or the king, the response would have been five hearts and...'

Waiting to hear no more, Molly led the ♣Q.

The Chimp went up with the ♣A and the Hog ruffed. On a trump to dummy's ace, Molly threw a club. At trick three, the Chimp played the ♣K on another club from dummy and again the Hog ruffed. Next came a trump to the ♣10 and a third club ruff, the Chimp this time shedding a heart.

What, I wondered, would H.H. do next? He would draw trumps... and then? A finesse in diamonds was, of course, the better proposition, for if it lost a 3-3 break would still bring home the contract and if that, too, failed to materialize, the heart finesse would still be available. All in all, the contract was a long odds-on chance.

'Everything's wrong,' whispered the Owl who had carried out a reconnaissance round the table. 'Every card.'

Unlike Molly, I thought, the Hog could then plead genuine bad luck. I was still trying to work out the odds in favor of the slam when he suddenly produced the ♠2!

Charlie the Chimp looked at it incredulously. The one card in his hand which he hadn't expected would take a trick was the ♠5. After grimacing and talking to himself, as was his wont, he returned the ◇3. The Hog captured Molly's ◇9 with dummy's ◇J, cashed the ◇A and continued with a lead to his ◇K. When Molly showed out, throwing a club, he glanced around him to make sure that he had an audience and with a flourish spread his hand.

'You are conceding one down?' inquired M.M.

The Hog feigned surprise. 'My dear Molly,' he replied in shocked tones, 'I didn't want to insult you by going through the motions, but you can see, I am sure, that the king of hearts must now fall. When, after eight spades and three diamonds, you come down to two cards one of them must be a club for the eight of clubs is still in dummy. I discard it on my last trump and the heat is on Charlie who must keep a diamond. Neither of you, therefore, can retain a guard for the king of hearts and dummy's queen of hearts becomes my twelfth winner.'

This was the deal in full:

```
                    ♠ A 10
                    ♡ A Q 10 5
                    ◊ A J 5
                    ♣ 8 7 4 3
    ♠ —                             ♠ 5 4 3
    ♡ 9 7 6 3          N            ♡ K J 8 4
    ♣ 9 4          W       E        ◊ Q 10 7 3
    ♣ Q J 10 9 6 5 2     S          ♣ A K
                    ♠ K Q J 9 8 7 6 2
                    ♡ 2
                    ◊ K 8 6 2
                    ♣ —
```

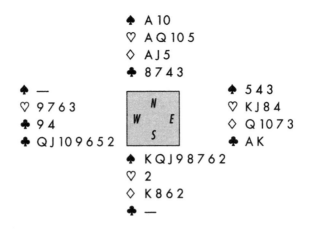

Quick to open a second front, Molly turned on the Chimp. 'Why,' she demanded to know, 'couldn't you return a heart instead of that ridiculous diamond? If only men had a speck of intuition!'

'It would have made no difference,' the Hog assured her. 'After cashing the ace and queen of hearts I would have ruffed a heart and now neither of you in the three-card ending could have kept three diamonds. The double squeeze would still be on.'

The kibitzers applauded, but Oscar the Owl had reservations. 'A very spectacular gambit that two of spades, H.H., but was it really necessary? Wouldn't you have arrived at the same position had you finessed the jack of diamonds as anyone else would have done?'

The Hog shook his head. 'You can say that because you know that the Chimp had four diamonds. What if the finesse loses to the doubleton queen and a heart comes back? Now Molly keeps the long diamond and a club while Charlie looks after the king of hearts. No squeeze left against anyone.'

'But this way, too,' persisted the Owl, 'Charlie might have had a doubleton queen of diamonds.'

'Certainly,' agreed the Hog 'but he would have to commit himself before I did. His return and the subsequent discards would have told me which squeeze to go for. If he plays back a heart, I cash the queen and ace and squeeze Molly in the minors, or else he is squeezed in the red suits himself. If he returns a diamond, I play as I did.'

'Of course,' added the Hideous Hog modestly casting down his eyelashes, 'a genius, sitting East, might return a low diamond from ◊Qx or the queen from ◊Qxxx. No declarer would see through that, but do you know of a defender who could rise to such heights? I can think of none — well, not more than one anyway.'

8. It's the Shock that Does the Damage

'If I wanted to amass masterpoints, which Heaven forbid,' the Hog was saying, 'I would choose the most involved and complex system available, one that would perplex partner part of the time and opponents all the time, giving me the edge in confusion. I might even take up that new-fangled Polish code, where you pass if you have a bid and bid if you haven't.'

'But...' began Oscar the Owl, our senior Kibitzer.

'Not at all,' retorted H.H. sharply. 'Opponents do not have the chance to play against such extravaganzas often enough to punish them effectively. Besides it irritates them and that's always a good thing. It's not like rubber bridge where an untutored partner would be the first victim. Playing for money a contented partner is more valuable than bad-tempered opponents. If I so often play Precision these days,' went on H.H., 'it's not because of all the savant gadgets that you can foist on it, but because it keeps partner happy when you don't and so you are much less likely to have a catastrophe.

'Admittedly,' continued the Hog, refilling his glass, 'one disaster is rarely crippling by itself. It's those that follow that are so expensive. Yes,' added H.H., casting his mind back to the afternoon's match. 'It's the shock of a big penalty, not the amount that does the damage. It's demoralizing.'

We were discussing over a magnum at the Griffins Club after a money match between Papa's Dinosaurs and the Hog's Pterodactyls. Oscar the Owl had missed the play and we were telling him how, after building up a huge lead, the Dinosaurs suddenly collapsed and lost the match on the last board.

'This is the deal which swung the match,' the Hog was saying. 'We'll play back the record and you can make the fateful decision, Oscar. You are North:

♠ 5 4 3   ♡ K Q 8 7 6 4   ◊ J 2   ♣ K 8

Both sides are vulnerable. Partner opens one diamond and West comes in with three spades. What action do you take?'

Oscar blinked. Picking up the Bollinger out of the bucket, the Hog gave him plenty of time to think. Then he resumed: 'Do you bid four hearts? Yes or no?'

'I don't like it,' said the Owl nodding his head. 'It could cost 500 or even 800. And yet, if I pass and we miss game that, too, would cost 620 or 650, and since I've little by way of defense, they are quite likely to make their contract. All in all, passing can be just as expensive as bidding.'

'So?' persisted H.H.

'On balance,' ventured O.O., 'bidding four hearts is perhaps the lesser risk. After all, partner is unlimited. He could have nineteen or even twenty points, and yet, with an undistinguished doubleton in hearts, he could hardly double. It's up to me. I bid four hearts. What happens?

Filling in the diagram, the Hog showed him:

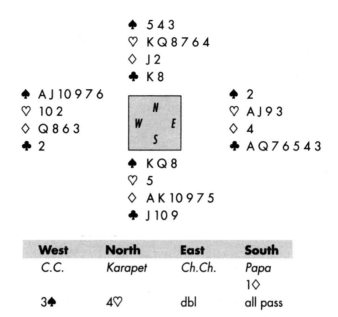

```
              ♠ 5 4 3
              ♡ K Q 8 7 6 4
              ◇ J 2
              ♣ K 8
♠ A J 10 9 7 6                    ♠ 2
♡ 10 2            N               ♡ A J 9 3
◇ Q 8 6 3    W       E            ◇ 4
♣ 2              S                ♣ A Q 7 6 5 4 3
              ♠ K Q 8
              ♡ 5
              ◇ A K 10 9 7 5
              ♣ J 10 9
```

West	North	East	South
C.C.	Karapet	Ch.Ch.	Papa
			1◇
3♠	4♡	dbl	all pass

'The Chimp doubled gleefully and led his singleton spade to the Corgi's ace. Back came a club, and after cashing the ace and queen, the Chimp led another for the Corgi to ruff with the heart ten. Overruffing wouldn't help, so Karapet threw a spade, but he couldn't avoid losing three more tricks and so, you see, your lesser risk came to 1100. That was bad enough, but it so unnerved poor Karapet that he misplayed the next hand and misdefended the one after, and...'

'But what has it to do with Precision?' broke in the Owl. 'A preemptive bid breaks the normal rhythm and this, you must agree, was a very unlucky hand. For all that, it could happen to anyone.'

'On the contrary,' rejoined the Hog 'it couldn't have happened to me. I had Karapet's hand in the other room, but playing Precision I knew, while he didn't, that partner had at most fifteen points and maybe as few as eleven. We couldn't be missing game unless we had a good fit, and if we had one, so would they, and their suit was higher-ranking than ours. Your 'lesser risk', knowing so little about partner's hand, was to go down 1100. Mine, with much more to go on, was to pass and collect 100. It makes all the difference, you see,' added H.H., 'to know what partner *can't* have.'

Oscar
the Owl

A Flaw in the System

'Mind you' went on the Hog, 'no system can cater for every hand as the last board was to show. By then, I, er, we had nearly made up for the blunders and bloomers in the other room and were only some 200 points behind. You can sit South with Papa on this occasion. Here we are:

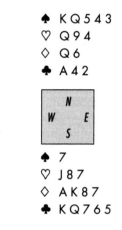

♠ K Q 5 4 3
♥ Q 9 4
♦ Q 6
♣ A 4 2

♠ 7
♥ J 8 7
♦ A K 8 7
♣ K Q 7 6 5

West	North	East	South
C.C.	Karapet	Ch.Ch.	Papa
pass	1♠	pass	2♣
pass	2♠	pass	3♦
pass	3♥	pass	3NT
all pass			

The Corgi led a heart to the Chimp's ace. A lead back to the king of hearts was followed by another heart, leaving Papa in dummy with the queen. Crossing to the king of clubs he led a spade, dummy's king winning. What next?'

The Owl looked for the catch but couldn't find one. 'The ace of clubs, I suppose,' he hazarded reluctantly. 'What else?'

The Hog nodded. 'That's what Papa did. The Corgi showed out and now,' pursued H.H., filling in the East-West hands, 'it only took Papa another minute to go down and three more to plead bad luck.'

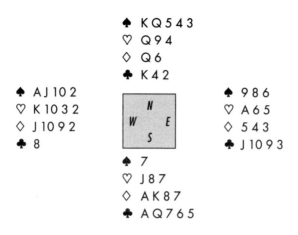

```
                    ♠ K Q 5 4 3
                    ♡ Q 9 4
                    ◇ Q 6
                    ♣ K 4 2
♠ A J 10 2                              ♠ 9 8 6
♡ K 10 3 2          N                   ♡ A 6 5
◇ J 10 9 2      W       E               ◇ 5 4 3
♣ 8                    S                ♣ J 10 9 3
                    ♠ 7
                    ♡ J 8 7
                    ◇ A K 8 7
                    ♣ A Q 7 6 5
```

'And what has Precision got to do with it this time?' asked O.O. suspiciously.

'But for the system,' explained the Hideous Hog, 'I, too, would have rebid two spades over two clubs and over three diamonds, instead of that fatuous three hearts, I would have bid three notrump. Playing Precision my opening had already shown a five-card spade suit, so I couldn't rebid it, not just like that. Raising R.R.'s suit is obviously futile, and a two notrump rebid promises much more than I had, so I was left with two hearts. At worst, I thought, if he raised me we would be on a 4-3 fit with the lead coming up to the stronger player. Unfortunately, this allowed the Rabbit, contrary to all my teaching, to bid three notrump. He knows perfectly well that he is strictly forbidden to bid notrump, unless it's clear that I shall play the hand in something else. But there it was. Taking advantage of a flaw in the system, he got the better of me.'

'But you won the match just the same,' protested O.O., 'so presumably he made three notrump.'

'That's quite beside the point,' replied the Hog. 'Instead of winning the match by good play, with myself at the wheel, we won it by a fluke, an accident, a misadventure, a...'

'How did the defense slip up?' asked the Owl, finding it all very confusing.

Taking up the story, I told him the defense had been identical in both rooms. After three rounds of hearts, the Rabbit came to hand with the ♣K and led a spade to dummy's king, just as Papa had done. It came out in the post mortem that he could now see ten tricks — five clubs, three diamonds, and the two tricks in the majors which he had scored already. All that remained was to go through the motions. The exact sequence of play didn't seem to matter much, so he began with a lead to ♣Q. When the Walrus, who was West, showed out, a derisive tutting noise from a junior kibitzer brought him up with a jolt. The tenth trick had suddenly vanished, taking two others with it. Having inadvertently blocked the clubs, his only remaining hope of a ninth trick was to drop the ◇ J109 in three rounds. With tremulous fingers R.R. began to cash his winners, starting with the ace of clubs. He was already gathering the trick when he realized that W.W. hadn't played to it. Walter the Walrus was frowning and thinking hard, but he couldn't escape.

On the second round of clubs he had shed the ♠10 but what could he spare now? If he parted with the ♠J, a conspicuous card which the Rabbit could hardly overlook, a low spade from dummy would bring down the ♠A, and the ◇Q would still be there as an entry. To let go a diamond would be disastrous. With a growl, the Walrus threw the thirteenth heart. Alas it didn't help the Rabbit, who was still short of a winner. Ruefully he cashed his diamonds, the Walrus following deceptively with the ◇2, the ◇10 and the ◇J. Was the Rabbit's ◇8 now good? He didn't think so, but any chance was better than none and the ♠4 didn't look remotely like a winner.

Stoically the Rabbit played his ◇8, but as he had feared all along, the ◇9 was still out. Winning the trick the Walrus exited with the ♠J. With tremulous fingers the Rabbit went up with dummy's ♠Q and shut his eyes. When he opened them again he had made the contract and the Pterodactyls had won the match.

'Curious hand,' observed O.O. 'The defense can beat the hand by ducking the first heart, but once they have failed to do that the key to success lies in blocking the clubs; West is squeezed only if he has to find a second discard while dummy still has two entries. If the clubs are played normally, he can afford to bare his ace of spades, for with the queen of diamonds as his only entry, declarer cannot bring down the ace of spades and get back to score the queen of diamonds. Would you have found this inspired misplay of the clubs, H.H.? If not', concluded the Owl, 'this is surely an even better hand for the system than the one before.'

9. Anyone Can Make a Mistake

'There must always be a first time,' said Oscar the Owl, our Senior Kibitzer.

'A superficial view,' retorted the Hideous Hog. 'Everything has happened before, everything that matters, that is. I'm not thinking of space travel, or new forms of pollution, or computerized cooking, or.....'

'But if it hasn't happened to us,' broke in Peregrine the Penguin, 'then it is the first time and with no previous experience to guide us we don't know how best to handle it.'

'Then,' rejoined the Hog, 'we must put to good use the experience of others.'

We were discussing defense against weak two-bids. No one at the Griffins had ever met them, but recently two distinguished overseas visitors, a Laplander and a Saudi, in pinstriped trousers with CD plates on their cars, have been using them regularly. With no suitable countermeasures at our disposal, we have often been led into costly indiscretions or else we've allowed ourselves to be crowded out of the bidding.

'It's the first time for us,' pursued the Hog, 'but don't forget that in America weak two-bids are as common as handguns. Have been for years, so all we have to do is to select their best weapons.'

'And which are they?' asked O.O.

'The best are always the simplest,' replied H.H. 'It took me three minutes to master the Precision treatment, so let's say it would take the average player ten minutes. I gave Wei and Andersen's *Profits from Preempts* to the Rabbit and even he couldn't go wrong when I put him through the catechism.'

'And what about the Standard American method?' inquired P.P.

'I've no idea,' replied the Hog. 'It is not in the nature of things for Standard American to do anything simple if it can be made complicated. I'm sure they've found a way. I chose the Precision method because, as S. J. Simon used to say of Acol, it's not so much a system as an attitude of mind. Yes,' went on H.H., 'the two have a lot in common, you know. Acol's salient feature is the limit bid which tells the opener where the balance of strength lies as soon as he hears partner's response. Precision carries it further with the opening itself limiting the hand.'

'But what has that to do with defensive bidding?' asked the Penguin.

'The same principle is at work,' replied the Hog. 'The objective is to describe a holding as fully as possible at the first opportunity. Take your weak two-bid. The standard defense is to treat it exactly as you would a one-bid. And that's just what it isn't, for it deprives the other side of a vital round of bidding. If you double two spades and hear three hearts you don't know whether partner has anything or nothing. The margin of uncertainty could extend to eight points or so. There's no room, as in responding to a one bid, to show moderate encouragement without going to game. It's all or nothing.'

'So?' inquired the Owl.

'So,' explained the Hog 'the Precision method is to introduce a Sign-off. With a useless hand, responder to the double calls two notrump and the doubler bids three clubs. Now responder plays in his suit at the three-level. It follows that if the response is not two notrump it's constructive.'

'You can no longer use two notrump as natural,' objected the Penguin.

'True,' agreed the Hog, 'but that rarely leads to game unless the doubler has something to say. And if responder has a bit more himself, he can call three notrump. All in all, you gain a lot more on the swings than you lose on the roundabouts.'

It wasn't long before two deals, one at rubber bridge, the other in a pairs event, put the Precision mechanism to the test. Both times the Hog was playing with the Rabbit. This was the first occasion:

North-South Vul.
Dealer East

```
            ♠ 5
            ♡ 7 4 3 2
            ◇ 10 4
            ♣ Q 10 9 7 5 2
```

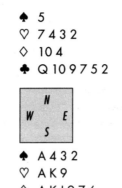

```
            ♠ A 4 3 2
            ♡ A K 9
            ◇ A K J 9 7 6
            ♣ —
```

West	North	East	South
Lapp	*R.R.*	*Saudi*	*H.H.*
		2♠	dbl
pass	2NT	pass	3♣
dbl	all pass		

Momentarily, the Hog toyed with the idea of passing 2NT. Since the Rabbit clearly had some sort of weedy club suit, opponents couldn't run it and in notrump there would be one trick fewer to make. In clubs however, the Hog would be at the wheel. In notrump it would be the Rabbit and the difference certainly came to more than one trick. So H.H. manfully did his duty.

This was the deal in full:

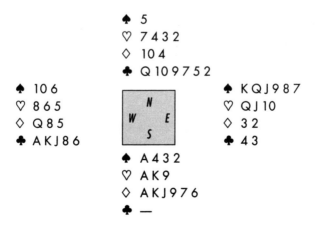

```
                    ♠ 5
                    ♡ 7 4 3 2
                    ◇ 10 4
                    ♣ Q 10 9 7 5 2
♠ 10 6                              ♠ K Q J 9 8 7
♡ 8 6 5                             ♡ Q J 10
◇ Q 8 5                             ◇ 3 2
♣ A K J 8 6                         ♣ 4 3
                    ♠ A 4 3 2
                    ♡ A K 9
                    ◇ A K J 9 7 6
                    ♣ —
```

West led the ♣A, East following with the ♣3, the Hog discarding a diamond. West switched to the ♠10. With five top tricks in the side suits, the Hog needed to score four trumps in dummy for his contract, so he began by ruffing a spade. Nothing was going to help if the Saudi had a singleton diamond, so the Hog continued by cashing the two top diamonds and ruffing another spade.

This was now the position:

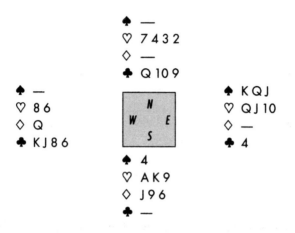

It was but a simple matter to cash the ♡A and ♡K, ruff a diamond, and exit with one of dummy's hearts. Nothing could prevent the ♣Q from becoming the Hog's ninth trick.

'An interesting hand,' observed the Hog. 'You can make three diamonds, of course, or two notrump, for that matter, but how do you get there? Hearing three clubs in response to his double, wouldn't any self-respecting South bid three notrump? And the others, too, if it comes to that? It's a useful gadget, that Precision mechanism. Why, I might have invented it myself.'

Two or three days later in the weekly duplicate at the Unicorn, the Hog found himself in a very similar situation. His holding, again with a void in clubs, was:

♠ K 9   ♡ A J 8 3   ◇ A K Q J 10 7 6   ♣ —

The Saudi, East, once more, opened 2♠, the Hog doubled and the Rabbit made the conventional response of 2NT. This time the Hog didn't hesitate. That the clubs were stopped was all he needed to know. Eight top tricks and the ♠K on the right side should be more than enough for the least gifted declarer to make 3NT.

East, as expected, led a spade. The ♠K held and the Rabbit quickly proceeded to wrap up thirteen tricks, for this was the deal:

Both Vul.
Dealer East

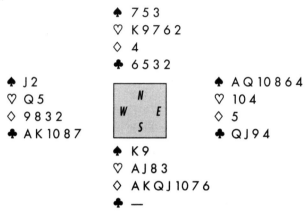

```
                    ♠ 7 5 3
                    ♡ K 9 7 6 2
                    ◊ 4
                    ♣ 6 5 3 2
    ♠ J 2                          ♠ A Q 10 8 6 4
    ♡ Q 5              N           ♡ 10 4
    ◊ 9 8 3 2      W      E        ◊ 5
    ♣ A K 10 8 7       S           ♣ Q J 9 4
                    ♠ K 9
                    ♡ A J 8 3
                    ◊ A K Q J 10 7 6
                    ♣ —
```

'A club lead would have defeated the contract,' observed a junior kibitzer.

'Anyone can make a mistake,' replied the Hog, licking his chops. 'Why, I nearly made one myself once.'

10. Sinning in Safety

We were dining at the Griffins.

'Don't you find, R.R., that playing Precision inhibits the Hog's natural game?' asked Oscar the Owl, our senior kibitzer.

The Rabbit sipped his Rosé d'Anjou and gazed thoughtfully at his artichoke before replying.

'No, far from it,' he said after due consideration. 'He is just as unpredictable whatever he plays.'

'But surely the system restricts his flights of fancy,' persisted the Owl. 'There are certain disciplines...'

The Rabbit shook his head. 'The system, he always says, is a servant, not a master. If he does something 'wrong' it's not really wrong because he knows it's not correct, if you see what I mean.'

Sensing that he could, perhaps, have expressed himself more clearly, R.R. went on to explain.

'When the Toucan or the Walrus or I myself, for that matter, do something wrong it's because we think it's right. We know no better. So we come unstuck. Precision keeps us in check by reducing our errors to a minimum. But the Hog doesn't need be kept in check. Always a move or two ahead, he knows exactly what will happen next and then it needn't happen at all. Now take that hand I was telling you about...'

The deal in question had come up the previous day. I kibitzed it from a post of vantage between the Rueful Rabbit and Karapet, the Free Armenian, the most consistently unlucky player West of the Urals — and to the East of them, too, of course.

Both Vul.
Dealer South

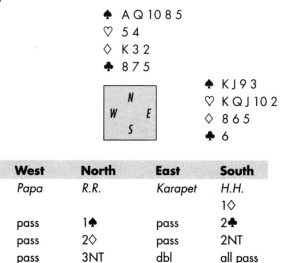

	♠ A Q 10 8 5
	♡ 5 4
	◇ K 3 2
	♣ 8 7 5

♠ K J 9 3
♡ K Q J 10 2
◇ 8 6 5
♣ 6

West	North	East	South
Papa	R.R.	Karapet	H.H.
			1◇
pass	1♠	pass	2♣
pass	2◇	pass	2NT
pass	3NT	dbl	all pass

Instead of a spade lead, as expected, Papa the Greek led the ♣K, followed by the ♣Q, then the ♣J. All held. The Armenian signalled with the ♡K, next he discarded the ♠3. At trick four, Papa switched to the ♡9, overtaken by the ♡10 and captured by the Hog with the ♡A. Five top diamonds and the ace of clubs followed rapidly. Papa's three discards were the ♠7, the ♣2, then the ♡3.

Anticipating the three-card ending, Karapet could feel the Sword of Damocles grazing his Adam's apple. Marked on his double with the ♠K, the throw-in was inevitable. There was one chance and one only of averting it, but it was a good one. Papa had discarded high-low in spades, showing an even number, so the Hog's shape was clearly 2-2-5-4. Unless his second heart happened to be the eight, Nemesis could be side-stepped by a far-seeing unblocking play. Karapet duly jettisoned his high hearts, coming down to the ♡2 and the ♠KJ.

Thereupon the Hog spread his hand. The full deal was:

```
                    ♠ A Q 10 8 5
                    ♡ 5 4
                    ◇ K 3 2
                    ♣ 8 7 5
♠ 7 6 4 2                              ♠ K J 9 3
♡ 9 3              ┌─────────┐         ♡ K Q J 10 2
◇ 9 7          W   │    N    │   E     ◇ 8 6 5
♣ K Q J 10 9       │    S    │         ♣ 6
                   └─────────┘
                    ♠ —
                    ♡ A 8 7 6
                    ◇ A Q J 10 4
                    ♣ A 4 3 2
```

'I demanded a spade lead!' cried Karapet.

'Then why signal with the king of hearts?' retorted Papa. 'I showed you four spades, so why didn't you throw all yours away?'

'You showed me two spades,' protested the Armenian. 'Did you really expect me to place him with a void? What abominable bidding!'

'You see,' said the Rabbit when he came to the end of the story. 'I wouldn't have dared to bid notrump with a void in partner's suit — after a sign-off, too. But the Hog does these things no matter what system he plays.'

'It's not a true Precision sequence,' objected the Owl.

'Of course not,' agreed R.R., 'but it's no worse in Precision than in anything else and it shows that the system doesn't inhibit the Hog. It provides a sound structure, but doesn't rule out extramural activities when the fancy takes him.'

'If you want a more clearly defined systemic example,' went on the Rabbit, discarding the last leaf of his artichoke, 'I can show you a hand from Thursday's duplicate at the Unicorn...'

The Better Sinner Takes Charge

'It's no use playing the averages,' I heard H.H. tell R.R. as they waited for Walter the Walrus and Molly the Mule on the last set of boards. 'To make it a winning score we need a top or two.'

Neither Vul.
Dealer South

```
                  ♠ 9 4 2
                  ♡ A 10 3
                  ◇ Q J 8 4
                  ♣ A J 3
  ♠ A 10 8 5                      ♠ K Q J
  ♡ Q 9 8 5           N          ♡ 7 6 4 2
  ◇ 3            W         E      ◇ 9 2
  ♣ 10 7 5 4          S          ♣ Q 9 8 6
                  ♠ 7 6 3
                  ♡ K J
                  ◇ A K 10 7 6 5
                  ♣ K 2
```

West	North	East	South
W.W.	R.R.	M.M.	H.H.
			1◇
pass	2◇	pass	2♠
pass	3♠	pass	3NT
all pass			

When the bidding was over, the Hog and the Rabbit were questioned closely about the meaning of the Precision sequence.

'Yes,' agreed the Hog, 'the two diamonds was forcing.'

'And what did two spades mean?' asked the Walrus.

'That,' explained the Rabbit, 'showed a control in spades but not in hearts.'

'What do you understand by the raise to three spades?' inquired Molly suspiciously.

'The purpose is to steer the contract into my hand,' replied H.H.

'In case the spade control is, say, Kx or Kxx,' added R.R. helpfully.

'Couldn't it be a suit?' persisted Molly.

'No,' explained the Hog. 'Playing Precision we rarely lose a major. If R.R. had four spades he would have responded one spade, not two diamonds.'

With these preliminaries out of the way, the Walrus led the ♡5. A spade would come best from the other side, through declarer, he thought.

Having to follow to nine red winners was a chore, but Molly was in no real trouble. Since the Hog's spade control could only be the ace, he couldn't have the ♣K as well, for that would give him an 18-count, a 1♣ opening with two points to spare. So, without a care in the world, she bared her ♣Q and the Hog duly collected twelve tricks for an undisputed top.

Muttering something unflattering abut 'these men', Molly looked for the Tournament Director. The Walrus threatened a writ. Eventually, both thought better of it — though not of the Hog.

'Consider the course things would have taken had we been playing some other system,' said H.H., when we discussed the hand later in the bar. 'The response to my one diamond would have been three diamonds which I would have converted to three notrump, as it was at other tables, but playing Precision I had an advantage in that I could make an inhibitory bid without running the slightest risk. The system doesn't encourage psychics, but if I can mislead opponents without confusing partner, why not?'

'We can sin in safety,' explained the Rabbit. 'Only the Hog is, of course, a much better sinner than I am, so I leave it to him.'

11. The Rabbit Counts up to Three

We were dining at the Griffins.

'So you see,' declared the Hog, glass aloft, 'he's utterly selfish and a miser into the bargain.' He said no more until he had despatched the last of the *chateaubriand à la planche*, but we knew all along what had made him so cross. Walter the Walrus had told us his side of the story before dinner. A new book on Precision had just come out and the Hog had asked W.W. to lend him his copy in the usual way. Claiming that the Hog never returned borrowed books, the Walrus refused point blank.

Oscar the Owl, our Senior Kibitzer, put the Walrus's case.

'Untrue,' protested the Hog. 'Only the other day I gave him back within the hour a book on Standard American.'

'Who wouldn't?' murmured Colin the Corgi, the facetious young man from Oxbridge.

Ignoring him, the Hog went on. 'What if I did lose some silly book of his once? Would it have killed him to buy a second copy?'

'One naturally avoids going to extremes,' ventured the Corgi, 'but couldn't you have bought the book yourself?'

'Unlike some of you,' retorted the Hog with spirit, 'I'm a busy man. I can't spend all day browsing through bookshops. This time, fortunately, it won't be necessary. The Rabbit bad the forethought to purchase a spare copy, but that's not the point. Refusing to lend a fellow member a book is unclubbable, to say the least. It shows a mean, ugly streak. It... oh, sommelier...'

The approach of the wine waiter created a welcome diversion and the Owl seized the chance to break in.

'What's this book about?' he asked.

'I won't know till I've seen it, will I?' replied the Hog, 'and that odious Walter...'

'But it might be about one of those ingenious gadgets that you never tire of denouncing,' persisted O.O.

'And I never will,' agreed H.H. 'I play to win and I like to enjoy myself in the process and no code or cipher has so far added a cent to my income. But I'm no blinkered doctrinaire either and if some gadget helps to bring in the money without robbing me of the pleasure in getting it, I've no objection to it at all. Is a gadget simple, that's the test.'

'And who's to say whether a gadget is or isn't simple?' asked O.O.

'The Rabbit, of course,' promptly rejoined the Hog. 'If he doesn't get confused, nobody will. And even he, you know, can count up to three — well, some of the time, anyway. Let me show you a hand I had with him a few days ago. It was the first time we tried out trump asking bids.'

Moving to the side his glass of *Romanée Conti*, the Hog scribbled quickly on the tablecloth:

$$\spadesuit 2 \quad \heartsuit A Q 7 6 4 \quad \diamondsuit Q 10 5 \quad \clubsuit Q 7 3 2$$

'There' he said. 'Partner opens one club. Opponents keep quiet.'

'Bid one heart,' said O.O.

'Partner bids two hearts, a trump asking bid.'

The Owl nodded sagely. 'Yes, I know. The reply is by steps. To show a five-card suit with two top honours you call three clubs.'

'Having counted up to three,' pursued H.H., 'the Rabbit, for he it is who's your partner, bids three spades. Your move.'

'If I'm not mistaken.' replied O.O., 'a new suit after the response to a trump asking bid enquires about controls, so I bid four diamonds, three steps showing the king or a singleton. What comes next?'

'The Rabbit soars straight into six hearts,' said H.H.

There was a pause. 'What lead did you get?' asked the Owl politely.

'If it's not on the secret list, may we see dummy?' suggested the Corgi.

'You may, when the bidding is over,' rejoined the Hog. 'Meanwhile, with thirteen winners in sight, I bid seven hearts.'

'Which thirteen winners?' asked the Corgi. 'We've answered a couple of questions, but what do we know of partner's hand?'

The Hog greeted the remark with a supercilious smile. 'You know all you need to know, my dear Colin,' he assured the Corgi. 'Consider. The trumps are solid, otherwise partner wouldn't be asking questions. In spades he has the ace, but no king, so...'

'Why not two small spades with the ace-king in the minors to make up the points?'

'Because,' explained H.H. 'if the Rabbit had, say, six hearts and no loser in the minors we'd be on the way to the grand slam. In fact we'd have got there by now. And if there is a loser in either minor my queen will provide the thirteenth trick.'

'A minor-suit king could be missing,' objected O.O.

'A further asking bid would have quickly cleared that up,' replied H.H. 'All the machinery is there — without having to count beyond three,' he added with a meaningful look.

Shifting a plate and a couple of spoons the Hog made room for the full diagram:

Both Vul.
Dealer East

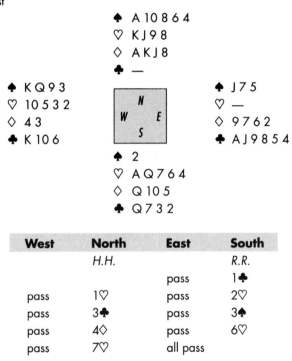

	♠	A 10 8 6 4
	♡	K J 9 8
	◇	A K J 8
	♣	—

♠ K Q 9 3		♠ J 7 5
♡ 10 5 3 2		♡ —
◇ 4 3		◇ 9 7 6 2
♣ K 10 6		♣ A J 9 8 5 4

	♠	2
	♡	A Q 7 6 4
	◇	Q 10 5
	♣	Q 7 3 2

West	North	East	South
	H.H.		R.R.
		pass	1♣
pass	1♡	pass	2♡
pass	3♣	pass	3♠
pass	4◇	pass	6♡
pass	7♡	all pass	

'The lead is the king of spades,' said H.H.

'We have ten top tricks,' mused the Owl. 'Three club ruffs in dummy would bring the total to thirteen.'

'True,' agreed the Hog, 'but we must allow for the existing 4-0 trump break, so we can't afford to expend an honor on a club ruff. After the spade ace at trick one we ruff a spade. That should be automatic. Next we lay down the ace of hearts and discover the bad trump break. Another trump, finessing the nine, and we ruff a second spade. Crossing with a diamond, we ruff a third spade with the queen of trumps, and going back to dummy with a second diamond we draw trumps. The fifth spade is a trick and we've made our grand slam on a combined count of twenty-six with nothing longer than a five-card suit around.'

'A dummy reversal *en passant*' suggested the Corgi.

12. Monster Points

While the text of this story has appeared in other books, the deals that accompany this version have not — Ed.

'Master Points!' scoffed the Hideous Hog. 'Why, the whole idea is unnatural.'

H.H. was not in a good mood. His doctor had told him to lose twenty pounds — or rather not to put on another twenty — and he was dieting rigorously. No refreshment between tea and dinner, *foie gras* on weekdays only, and no carbohydrates except bread and potatoes. Unaccustomed to privations, the Hog was taking a jaundiced view of life.

'Why unnatural?' enquired Oscar the Owl, Senior Kibitzer at the Griffins.

'Because,' snapped the Hog, 'if you reward success, you should punish failure. The two go together.'

'Are you suggesting…?' began the Owl.

'Certainly I am' replied the Hog warmly. 'If you present Master Points for merit, you should inflict Monster Points for demerit. I have nothing against virtue, as such, but why should sin go unpunished? Minor peccadilloes don't come into it,' went on H.H. 'Anyone can be careless and miss some baby smother play or common trump squeeze. For that sort of thing a black mark or two would suffice. It's the enormities that call for special treatment.'

'But some enormities are more enormous than others,' objected O.O.

'Where would you draw the line? And who would do it?'

Thoughtfully, the Hog sipped my sherry. Having consumed his ration — his Spartan diet allowed two drinks only before dinner — he had ordered the barman to remove his glass. After a while he resumed: 'Anyone would be entitled to submit a claim on someone else's behalf, that is. Should the claim be contested, a panel of experts would arbitrate. But this wouldn't happen often. Most offences are clear-cut and the Club Secretary or Tournament Director would decide on the spot.

Now take that slam of Papa's with poor Karapet yesterday. Could anyone but an artist in reverse, so to speak, plan such a catastrophe? There's an incontestable Monster Point for you!'

That Papa should be the first to qualify for the Hog's Monster Points scheme came as no surprise to us. Only the Greek had the temerity to dispute the Hog's supremacy at the card table and *lèse majesté* was something which H.H. was not disposed to treat lightly. The day before, Papa had played the leading part in a dramatic rubber against the Hideous Hog and Walter the Walrus. His partner was Karapet Djoulikyan, the Free Armenian, the unluckiest player in modern times.

A Prepared Cuebid

Sitting South, Papa dealt himself:

♠ — ♡ 6 3 ◇ A K Q J 10 9 3 2 ♣ A Q 4

The auction was spirited from the start:

West	North	East	South
W.W.	Karapet	H.H.	Papa
			1◇
2♡	3♣	4♠	

It is the gift of seeing several moves ahead that is the hallmark of the true expert and before choosing his next bid Papa had followed the auction, step by step, to its predestined conclusion. A grand slam was a cast-iron certainty, so long as he could prevent a heart lead. This could only be achieved by stages. The first move was to call 5♡ over 4♠, a prepared cuebid, as he explained later. The Walrus passed and Karapet, more lugubrious than ever, called 6♣. The Hog had nothing to say and Papa's big moment had come. Without further ado he bid 7◇.

The Greek would have been the first to agree that a game and small slam bonus should never be jeopardized unless the odds in favour of a grand slam were at least 2-1. But the crux of the matter was that with two losing hearts he had no hope of the small slam bonus. It would be easier, by far, to make 7◇ than 6◇, for then it would be obvious to West that he had no hearts, so he would lead some other suit.

Walter the Walrus doubled, and Papa, who was hoping for just that, promptly redoubled to make assurance doubly sure. After the 5♡

cuebid, the jump to 7◊ and the redouble, how could anyone think of leading a heart?

This was the complete deal:

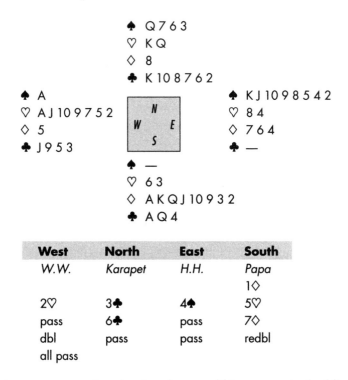

	♠ Q 7 6 3	
	♡ K Q	
	◊ 8	
	♣ K 10 8 7 6 2	

♠ A
♡ A J 10 9 7 5 2
◊ 5
♣ J 9 5 3

♠ K J 10 9 8 5 4 2
♡ 8 4
◊ 7 6 4
♣ —

♠ —
♡ 6 3
◊ A K Q J 10 9 3 2
♣ A Q 4

West	North	East	South
W.W.	Karapet	H.H.	Papa
			1◊
2♡	3♣	4♠	5♡
pass	6♣	pass	7◊
dbl	pass	pass	redbl
all pass			

The Walrus was not an imaginative player and his purpose in doubling 7◊ was to warn H.H. against attempting an unnecessary sacrifice. He had intended, of course, to lead the ♠A, until the redouble sowed doubt in his mind. Papa might have called a grand slam, gambling on a heart lead, for he clearly had no hearts but would he have redoubled if he had a losing spade? Surely not, and though it went against the grain to lead a club from his holding, no other suit was left. He had been cursed too often in the past for opening a singleton trump to try that again.

The Hog ruffed the club lead, returned a heart to W.W.'s ace and ruffed a second club. Three down.

'I make it 1600,' chortled the Hideous Hog 'or have I left out a nought somewhere?'

'They would have made a small slam,' I heard one junior kibitzer whisper to another, 'for of course West would try to cash his two aces.'

'He always does it to me, his best friend,' murmured Karapet sadly.

Walter the Walrus

'Just think of it!' lamented Papa. 'I create a vulnerable grand slam out of thin air. I earn a bonus of 1500, I stop a heart lead. And what happens? I run into an accursed void which no one could have foreseen. My luck is really out. I...'

'*Your* luck?' cried the outraged Armenian. He could take catastrophe in his stride for he was used to it. The Djoulikyans had known little else for generations. But that another should claim the credit for his bad luck, that was more than even Karapet could stand.

'I have had enough,' he declared in a voice choked with emotion. 'And kindly find another partner for tomorrow's duplicate at the Unicorn. You can have all the bad luck you like, so long as it isn't mine.'

The Hog mellowed a little as he recalled the deal. Other people's misfortunes, and more especially Papa's, tickled his fine sense of humor.

'Talking of Karapet,' he went on 'playing with that Walrus in the duplicate was very much a case of out of the frying pan into the fire. Ha! Ha! You tell them about it.' The Hog was otherwise engaged. There was no mention of olives on his diet and the barman had just set down another bowl before him.

ABOVE AND BELOW AVERAGE

Blinking his amber eyes, Oscar the Owl turned expectantly towards me. I had been the Hog's partner in the weekly duplicate at the Unicorn and this was one of our early boards:

Both Vul.
Contract: 4♡ by South

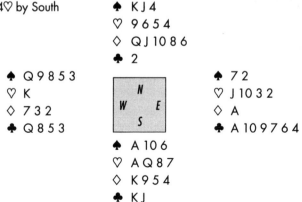

♠ K J 4
♡ 9 6 5 4
◊ Q J 10 8 6
♣ 2

♠ Q 9 8 5 3
♡ K
◊ 7 3 2
♣ Q 8 5 3

♠ 7 2
♡ J 10 3 2
◊ A
♣ A 10 9 7 6 4

♠ A 10 6
♡ A Q 8 7
◊ K 9 5 4
♣ K J

Winning the opening spade lead in his hand, the Hog laid down the ♡A. When the ♡K dropped, he led a low heart to dummy's nine and East's ten, finessing later against East's jack. The defenders scored their two aces and that was that.

'Somewhat above average' suggested the Hog as I picked up the traveling scoresheet. 'Not everyone will reach four hearts, though once you get there, you can't fail to make it, of course.'

The board had come to us from Table 13 where Karapet and the Walrus, sitting North-South, had played it against the Rueful Rabbit and Timothy the Toucan. The contract was again 4♡ by South but according to the scoresheet, ten tricks were made the other way, East-West scoring 700.

We called the Tournament Director. 'There's a mistake here,' we told him. 'Presumably we should read North-South for East-West, but what the 700 stands for isn't clear.'

'It's that Rabbit I expect,' said the Hog. 'How would he know East-West from North-South? Mind you, he shouldn't have been allowed near the scoresheet.'

After investigating, the Tournament Director came back to tell us that the result had been recorded correctly. This is what happened.

As at our table, the opening lead was a spade. Winning with the jack in dummy, the Walrus, who was declarer, took the heart finesse, losing to the Rabbit's lone ♡K. The spade continuation was won in the closed hand and now the Walrus laid down the ♡Q. We were not told what expression he gave to his injured feelings when the Rabbit showed out, but it is on record that he made no more tricks. After the ♡Q came a diamond. The Toucan won with the ace, drew trumps and led a low club. The Walrus misguessed and it was all over.

'With every card right,' remarked the Hog good-humoredly, when he heard the result. 'I shouldn't have thought it possible to go down at all without cheating. Perhaps Karapet should have stuck to Papa after all. Ha! Ha!'

All agreed that W.W.'s performance was out of the ordinary and deserved special mention.

Indeed, it has taken him to the head of the Monster Point table and a leading bookmaker has made him favorite in the race to be the first Life Monster.

13. An Unholy Match

With acknowledgements to Hugh Darwen, whose book Bridge Magic *contains a collection of the world's greatest double-dummy, sure trick and inferential problems. V.M.*

An owl hooted. A bat flew low over the long line of broomsticks parked outside the club. It was Halloween and the air was thick with witchcraft.

Disguised as Hugh Darwen, the famous double-dummy problemist, the sorcerer-in-chief slipped unnoticed into the cardroom of the Griffins. With eerie music from a witches' chorus in the background, he began to cast a spell, 'Abracadabra, abracadabra,' and soon the cards were dancing to his unearthly tune. The best contracts couldn't be made. The worst ones couldn't be defeated.

'Let's try a goulash,' suggested someone in desperation. If normal dealing produced crazy results, maybe a crazy deal would lead to a normal one.

'What's a goulash?' asked Timothy the Toucan.

'After a throw-in,' explained the Rueful Rabbit, 'the cards aren't shuffled or anything and are dealt three or four cards at a time, so you get freak hands and everyone holds wonderful cards, with lovely long suits, but of course, they don't break and everything's topsy-turvy. They play a lot of goulashes in Paris,' added R.R. by way of a character reference.

All agreed. Maybe a goulash would break the spell.

Walter the Walrus dealt himself a 22-point hand, sighed resignedly and passed. Predestined to go down, since every deal was bewitched, he bowed to his fate. All passed and the Toucan proceeded to deal a goulash.

Neither Vul.
Dealer North

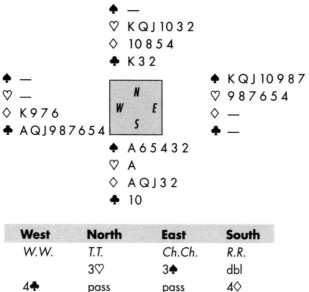

```
              ♠ —
              ♡ K Q J 10 3 2
              ◇ 10 8 5 4
              ♣ K 3 2

♠ —                         ♠ K Q J 10 9 8 7
♡ —              N          ♡ 9 8 7 6 5 4
◇ K 9 7 6    W     E        ◇ —
♣ A Q J 9 8 7 6 5 4   S     ♣ —

              ♠ A 6 5 4 3 2
              ♡ A
              ◇ A Q J 3 2
              ♣ 10
```

West	North	East	South
W.W.	T.T.	Ch.Ch.	R.R.
	3♡	3♠	dbl
4♣	pass	pass	4◇
5♣	5◇	pass	pass
dbl	all pass		

Walter the Walrus led the ♣A, then the four, a two-way card, as he explained later, partly suit preference, in case he got the chance to ruff a heart, and partly a promotion play. If, as he expected, declarer played low from dummy, he wanted partner to ruff.

The Rabbit duly played dummy's ♣3 and when Charlie the Chimp, sitting East, failed to ruff, R.R. sat bolt upright in his chair. Nostrils aquiver, ears twitching, he began to count. If the Chimp had neither clubs nor diamonds, his spades and hearts must add up to thirteen, and as he couldn't have more than seven spades, he simply had to have six hearts. From now on the hand could be played double-dummy.

If he drew trumps, ending on the table, he could unblock the hearts by jettisoning his ace on the ♣K, and score: four hearts, four trumps — losing one to the king — the ♠A and the ♣K, ten tricks all told. He could ruff a spade, of course, but then he couldn't bring in the hearts, for the Walrus would have a trump more than dummy.

Where, then, could he find the eleventh trick? Where would the Hog look for it?

A low, mocking chuckle echoed round the room.

'Let's put our heads together,' suggested Charlie the Chimp. 'We're all on the same side really tonight, aren't we? We've got to break the spell somehow.'

'Certainly,' agreed W.W. 'After all, everyone knows that I have ten points, so what is there to hide?'

'I'll be on your side, I mean our side, too,' promised the Toucan.

Fortifying himself with a sip of his brandy, the Rueful Rabbit soliloquized. 'I am only one trick short. It's the sort of thing that happens all the time, so...'

'Yes,' broke in the Chimp, 'only last Tuesday at the Unicorn...'

'The answer', went on R.R., ignoring the interruption, 'is usually a coup of some sort, a squeeze or...'

'You can't squeeze me' chipped in Charlie. 'I discard after dummy and anyway you've no communications.'

'How about a dummy reversal?' suggested the Rabbit. 'I've often seen the Hog do it when he's a trick short. He ruffs things in his hand and dummy's deuce draws the last trump. That sort of thing. Let's try it.'

As he spoke, he ruffed the ♣3 with the ◇Q.

'Must keep my low trumps as entries to dummy,' he explained. 'Otherwise, I will end up by throwing myself in.'

At trick three came the ◇J, ducked by the Walrus, then the ◇3. The Walrus was tempted to duck again, but he realized in time that he would then lose his king of trumps altogether. R.R. would throw his ♡A on the ♣K and lead hearts till W.W. ruffed. His best exit would be the ◇K, but dummy would now have a spare trump to ruff a spade and provide an entry, so declarer would have his eleven tricks — five diamonds, three hearts, the ♣K, the ♠A and a spade ruff.

Reluctantly, W.W. rose with the ◇K and returned a club.

'That's torn it,' exclaimed the Chimp. 'You can't unblock and cash dummy's hearts, for Walter would ruff and you can't draw trumps, for you've no way back to your hand.'

'Oh, haven't I?' retorted R.R. with spirit, lustily trumping the ♣K with his ◇A. 'There! Now I am in my hand and I'm going to finesse and reverse, that is, well...'

The ◇2, the rabbit's last trump came next, in this position:

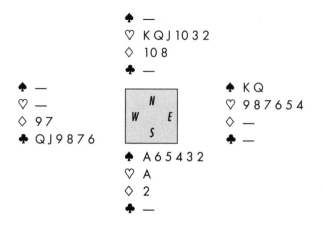

```
                    ♠ —
                    ♡ K Q J 10 3 2
                    ◇ 10 8
                    ♣ —
  ♠ —                              ♠ K Q
  ♡ —              ┌──────────┐    ♡ 9 8 7 6 5 4
  ◇ 9 7           │    N     │    ◇ —
  ♣ Q J 9 8 7 6   │ W     E  │    ♣ —
                   │    S     │
                   └──────────┘
                    ♠ A 6 5 4 3 2
                    ♡ A
                    ◇ 2
                    ♣ —
```

On the ◇8 the Chimp could let go a heart, but what could he discard on the ◇10? If he parted with another heart, R.R. would throw his ace of hearts and all dummy's hearts would be good. If he bared his ♠K, the Rabbit would come to his hand with the ♡A and score all his spades.

A toad croaked. With a patter of cloven feet on the marble staircase, the sorcerer fled in disarray, leaving behind him the smiling mask of Hugh Darwen.

14. The Hog and the Iced Water

'You'd better have some more iced water,' said the Hideous Hog, tipping the rest of the Montrachet '69 into his own glass. 'They'll nearly all be Americans on board and water's quite a thing with them, you know. To get into the swing of it, you should start practising now.'

'Then why are you drinking burgundy?' asked the Rueful Rabbit reproachfully. He had nothing against drinking water, or against any other eccentricity, but if he had to go into training months ahead to become a good mixer, why shouldn't the Hog do the same? Weren't they both going with all those Americans on the Vistafjord's Fall cruise to the Mediterranean?

'One's a prisoner of one's reputation,' replied H.H. with a sigh. 'Anyone looking me up in *Who's Who* or some other reference book will read: *Total abstainer from non-alcoholic beverages. Recreations: winetasting. Favorite sport: same.* I'd make myself conspicuous if I suddenly used water for drinking. It wouldn't be in good taste.' The Hog brushed the subject aside. 'Let's consider what system we'll play. That's much more important.'

The Rabbit opened his mouth.

'I wish you wouldn't always interrupt,' said the Hog severely. 'Where was I? Ah, yes, systems. You must remember that the Americans have more of everything that we have, more oil, more money and more points, many more. That's doubtless why they can afford to play the strong notrump. To confuse them we'll play the weak one.'

'You mean twelve to fourteen?' enquired R.R.

'Precisely' agreed H.H.. 'In your own case, however, it would be more prudent, perhaps, if you didn't bid notrump. Trick taking *per se* isn't the strongest part of your game, so on sketchy hands, pass, support me to the hilt and table your hand with confidence. Your dummy play,' added the Hog reassuringly, 'is above reproach. You lay your cards out so neatly.'

The Rabbit blushed.

'We'll play four-card majors,' went on the Hog, 'though you'd better have a five-card suit to do it with, just to have a bit in hand.'

'Now signaling. The Americans are very keen on it,' continued H.H., beckoning a passing waiter for more lobster salad.

'I thought that you were slimming,' broke in the Rabbit wincing as he sipped his iced water.

The Hog didn't hear him. 'Signaling' he repeated. 'You must learn the implications. There's more in it than meets the eye.'

'I know all about it,' R.R. assured him. 'I'll play high-low to show a doubleton or four and...'

'No, no,' interjected H.H. vigorously, 'after a trick or two I'll know what you have better than you will. So don't show anyone anything. Just look.'

'I don't understand,' began the Rabbit.

'Naturally,' agreed the Hog. 'I'll explain so that any paloo... any, er, person of high intelligence can grasp the point. Now take this hand I had the other day playing with the Walrus.' On the back of the wine list H.H. jotted down this hand.

Both Vul.
Dealer South

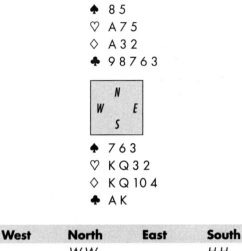

```
            ♠ 8 5
            ♡ A 7 5
            ◊ A 3 2
            ♣ 9 8 7 6 3

              N
           W     E
              S

            ♠ 7 6 3
            ♡ K Q 3 2
            ◊ K Q 10 4
            ♣ A K
```

West	North	East	South
	W.W.		H.H.
			1NT
pass	3NT	all pass	

'I opened one notrump, a routine percentage bid, giving me the best chance of becoming declarer. The Walrus raised to three notrump. West led the deuce of spades, finding East with ♠ AKJ9. I let go a heart from my hand and two hearts from dummy. At trick five came a nondescript heart from West. How do you play?'

The Rabbit nodded knowingly.

'Since you can't see it, I'll tell you,' went on the Hog. 'You have eight top tricks and therefore need the fourth diamond for your ninth. So you play for the drop or finesse against East's jack of diamonds as the situation demands.'

'And how do I find out what it demands?' asked the Rabbit suspiciously.

'By playing the ace-king of clubs, as I did' replied the Hog. The Rabbit's left ear twitched.

'Very well,' went on H.H.. 'I see that I'll have to spell it out in detail . You may be sure that each defender in turn will signal his club holding to the other, following high-low with two clubs or four and with the lowest from three.'

'How does that help?' asked the Rabbit.

'Count,' commanded the Hog, 'and don't forget the hearts, for you'll be cashing them in a moment or two. You'll know then how many cards East had in the majors. Suppose that he has two hearts only and signals three clubs. You know that he had four spades, so he must have four diamonds. Unless the jack drops, you take the marked finesse on the third round. If, as happened to be the case, East shows up with three hearts and three clubs, you can depend on diamonds breaking three-three.'

'But suppose that he has seven cards in hearts and clubs?' objected the Rabbit.

'Then,' replied the Hog, 'the contract is unmakeable, unless, of course, you're lucky enough to find a doubleton jack of diamonds. If, however, the contract depends on a guess, sending for a signal, so to speak, will help you to make the right guess.'

This was the full deal:

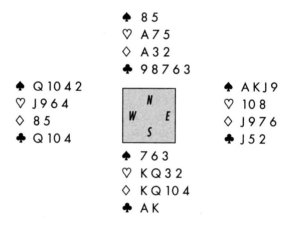

```
                    ♠ 8 5
                    ♡ A 7 5
                    ◇ A 3 2
                    ♣ 9 8 7 6 3
  ♠ Q 10 4 2          N          ♠ A K J 9
  ♡ J 9 6 4                      ♡ 10 8
  ◇ 8 5          W       E       ◇ J 9 7 6
  ♣ Q 10 4           S           ♣ J 5 2
                    ♠ 7 6 3
                    ♡ K Q 3 2
                    ◇ K Q 10 4
                    ♣ A K
```

The Hog scribbled busily on the menu. 'Here you are,' he said 'Test your technique on this one.'

Neither Vul.
Dealer South

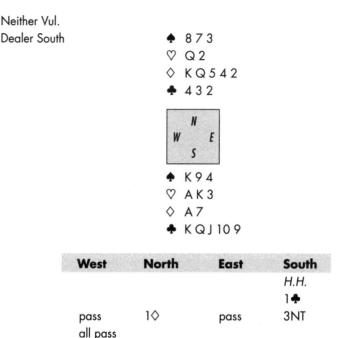

```
            ♠ 8 7 3
            ♡ Q 2
            ◇ K Q 5 4 2
            ♣ 4 3 2

                N
            W       E
                S

            ♠ K 9 4
            ♡ A K 3
            ◇ A 7
            ♣ K Q J 10 9
```

West	North	East	South
			H.H.
			1♣
pass	1◇	pass	3NT
all pass			

'I picked up the South hand a couple of days ago at duplicate and was lucky enough to be up against strong opponents who knew all about signaling. West led the five of spades to East's jack. You see the problem, don't you?'

'Of course,' said the Rabbit.

'Very well, then,' rejoined the Hog. 'I'll explain it in words of one syllable. If West started with four spades, I can set up my clubs. If he had five spades, I can't afford to lose the lead and my only chance will be a three-three diamond break. But if I test the diamonds first and they break 4-2, I may go down even if the spades are 4-3. I must guess, so what do I do?'

'Diamonds don't usually break 3-3,' observed the Rabbit.

'To find out,' went on the Hog, giving R.R. a withering look 'I led the seven of diamonds towards dummy. I was sure the defenders would tell each other how long to hold up the ace. When West produced the six and East the three, I went back to the ace of diamonds, crossed to the queen of hearts and cashed the rest of the diamonds, for as expected they broke 3-3. Had either East or West followed high-low, I would have had to abandon diamonds and switch to clubs, risking a 5-3 spade split.

'Simple enough' concluded H.H. 'so long as you can trust your opponents.'

'And what if you can't?' asked R.R. 'After all one can't always trust oneself, so how can one have so much faith in others?'

'Fortunately,' replied H.H. 'signalers are dedicated people, rather like Molière's doctors, who maintained that it was better for a patient to die after undergoing the correct treatment than to be cured by unorthodox methods. Signaling, you see, is an end in itself. Like virtue, it is its own reward.'

'Couldn't I send out some signals too?' persisted the Rabbit.

'It's not necessary,' rejoined H.H. 'You are by nature an egalitarian, my dear R.R., so you tend to treat all cards below honor rank as being equal. Your, er, distinctive style of playing the card nearest your thumb is confusing enough, so there's no need to signal. Of course there are occasions...'

The Hog was scribbling on the back of the bill.

North-South Vul.
Dealer West

```
              ♠ Q 9 8
              ♡ A 4
              ◇ A Q J 9
              ♣ A Q J 8
   ♠ 4 3                      ♠ A K 10 7 2
   ♡ 6 3          N           ♡ 7 5 2
   ◇ K 6 4 3 2  W   E         ◇ 8 7
   ♣ 9 7 6 4      S           ♣ K 5 2
              ♠ J 6 5
              ♡ K Q J 10 9 8
              ◇ 10 5
              ♣ 10 3
```

West	North	East	South
		H.H.	
pass	1◇	1♠	2♡
pass	3NT	pass	4♡
all pass			

'I was sitting East when this deal came up,' explained the Hog. 'Partner led the four of spades and I could see that we would need my king of clubs as the fourth trick to set the contract. Our third trick, of course, would be a spade ruff. Well, then, which spade do I lead at trick three?'

The Rabbit gurgled

'Exactly.' The Hog nodded sympathetically. 'It all depends on your estimate of declarer. It was easy in my case, for South was a fanatical signaler, so I led the ten of spades, an unnecessarily high card, clearly calling for a diamond. It meant nothing to partner, who returned a trump anyway. But declarer duly read my signal, and placing me with the king of diamonds took the club finesse. Against a less disingenuous declarer so obvious a play wouldn't work.'

'What card would you lead against a clever player like Papa?'

'The ten of spades might still be good card. He would reason that if I had king of diamonds I wouldn't be so foolish as to advertise it, so perhaps I really had it and was trying to bamboozle him.'

'And against me?' asked the Rabbit eagerly.

'It wouldn't matter,' replied the Hog sadly, 'for you wouldn't know which card I played.'

'Maybe,' said the Rabbit, grimacing as he drained his glass of iced water, 'it is better to know too little than too much. It's so frustrating for opponents.'

15. Madness in the Cards

'Genius, they say, is akin to madness, but it works the other way, too, you know,' said Oscar the Owl, our Senior Kibitzer at the Griffins.

Peregrine the Penguin, his opposite number at the Unicorn, nodded gravely.

'He's mad, undoubtedly,' he agreed, 'but it's his Guardian Angel who is the genius.

We were discussing the exploits of the Rueful Rabbit. Twice in one session, without malice aforethought, he had soared to brilliance on the wings of confusion.

On the first occasion, his Guardian Angel appeared in the unexpected guise of Charlie the Chimp, self-proclaimed humorist and inveterate chatterbox. This was the deal:

East-West Vul.
Dealer North

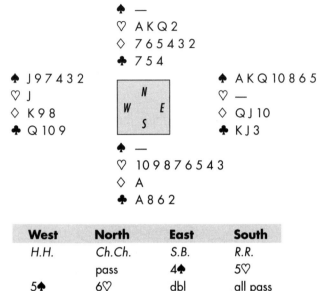

	♠ —	
	♡ A K Q 2	
	◇ 7 6 5 4 3 2	
	♣ 7 5 4	

♠ J 9 7 4 3 2
♡ J
◇ K 9 8
♣ Q 10 9

♠ A K Q 10 8 6 5
♡ —
◇ Q J 10
♣ K J 3

♠ —
♡ 10 9 8 7 6 5 4 3
◇ A
♣ A 8 6 2

West	North	East	South
H.H.	Ch.Ch.	S.B.	R.R.
	pass	4♠	5♡
5♠	6♡	dbl	all pass

There was nothing unusual about the bidding, but the Hog gave some
thought to the opening lead. It was certain that either declarer or dummy would have a void in spades and a distinct possibility that both had
voids, as above. A spade lead would therefore, present R.R. with a ruff
and discard. After due deliberation the Hog led the ♡J.

'If you can bid five hearts all on your own, you don't need trump
support from me,' began Charlie the Chimp, playfully putting down the
♡2 on his right, as if it were a singleton, and following slowly with the
diamonds, then the clubs, keeping back to the end the ♡AKQ.

'At favorable vulnerability and no defense...,' he prattled on mer-
rily.

The Rabbit wasn't listening. Mechanically he flicked the ♡2 on the
Hog's ♡J. As the Emeritus Professor of Bio-Sophistry, better known as
the Secretary Bird, played the ♣8, the Rabbit sat back apprehensively.
With so hopeless a dummy, he was prepared to go three or four down,
maybe five but now it looked as if he would go six down, at least, and
worse still, opponents would score 100 honors. He resented that 100
more than any of the others. It would cost the same but the humiliation
was infinitely greater.

The Rueful
Rabbit

Arithmetic had never been the Rabbit's best subject and before he worked out the likely penalty, the Chimp, smiling inanely, emerged at last with his three top hearts.

'Oh!' exclaimed the Rabbit, and again, more slowly, 'Oh!'

Dummy's card had been played and covered and it was too late to take it back.

'What a silly thing to do,' hissed the Secretary Bird. 'You think your monkey tricks are so funny, don't you? I'm sorry for your partner but it serves you right for being so childish.'

The Hideous Hog, who had been stroking his chin pensively, held up imperiously a fat, pink forefinger.

'This is a friendly game in a gentleman's club,' he began in his silkiest voice. 'We don't want to take advantage of a prank or a joke...'

'You have a duty to your partner,' broke in the Secretary Bird in hostile, sibilant tones. 'You have no right...'

The Hog waved him aside disdainfully. 'Take it back,' he urged the Rabbit with the air of a nobleman of old renouncing his *droit de seigneur*.

'No, no,' protested the Rabbit. 'I am as much to blame as Charlie. I shouldn't have played before the whole of dummy had been tabled.'

Turning to S.B., he went on with a touch of hauteur. 'You needn't worry, Professor. I am prepared to pay for my mistakes and I will accept no favors. I appreciate H.H.'s *beau geste*. Very sporting. But play on. I insist,' he added firmly.

The Hog's beady eyes narrowed and his purr gave way to a growl as reluctantly he led a spade. The Rabbit ruffed in his hand and laid down the ♢A. Crossing to dummy with the ♡A, then the ♡K he ruffed a diamond each time. Everyone seemed to follow and when the ♢K and ♢Q appeared on the third round, he was almost sure that dummy's three little diamonds were good. Going over the ♡Q he put it to the test. Yes, he was home.

'Amazing!' he exclaimed incredulously. 'To think that but for that silly nonsense at the first trick, I would have made a grand slam. Only goes to show.'

With hate in his eyes, the Hog glared at the Secretary Bird.

'At any rate, H.H.' observed Oscar the Owl, consolingly. 'You found the only lead to break the contract.'

Colin the Corgi, the facetious young man from Oxbridge, who had been kibitzing, had the last word.

'It wouldn't have occurred to a less inspired declarer,' he said, looking pityingly at the Rabbit, 'to duck the heart at trick one, and without that the contract is unmakeable. If one of the three top hearts is removed before the ace of diamonds has been played, dummy will be short of an entry. Declarer can still set up the suit, but he can no longer get back to enjoy it.' Turning to the Hog, he added, 'What a relief it must have been to you, H.H., that your *beau geste* didn't misfire.'

A CLASSICAL DEFENSE

The Guardian Angel was in action again a couple of rubbers later. This time, Papa the Greek and Timothy the Toucan faced the Rueful Rabbit and Walter the Walrus. Nothing much happened until this deal came up:

East-West Vul.
Dealer South

```
                    ♠ A 3
                    ♡ 9 8 7 6 5
                    ◇ Q 4 3
                    ♣ 4 3 2
   ♠ 10 4                              ♠ K 9 7 6 5
   ♡ Q                N                ♡ K J 10
   ◇ J 9 8 7 6 5 2  W   E              ◇ K 10
   ♣ J 9 5            S                ♣ K Q 8
                    ♠ Q J 8 2
                    ♡ A 4 3 2
                    ◇ A
                    ♣ A 10 7 6
```

West	North	East	South
W.W.	T.T.	R.R.	Papa
			1♠
pass	1NT	pass	2♡
pass	3♡	pass	3NT
pass	4♡	all pass	

While the Walrus debated with himself which card to lead, the Rabbit's mind wandered. It happened to him not infrequently. Where had he left his car? It couldn't be the usual place, behind the Unicorn, because he hadn't been there since Friday — or was it Thursday? No, Friday, because...

At this point W.W. led the ♠10 and the Toucan, bouncing gently as was his wont, tabled his hand, placing the spades on his right. It proved to be a fateful piece of dummy play.

As Papa played low from dummy, the Rabbit's heartbeats quickened, for wasn't this the classical situation he had seen in his textbook?

In the book, East calls 1♠ — yes, even the suit is the same — and South ends up in 3NT. West leads the top of the doubleton and declarer plays low from dummy, just as Papa had done. The inexperienced East rises with the ♠K, of course, the natural play, but the expert knows better. He encourages, but ducks. This is because West may gain the lead before East, and if so, he must have a spade left, so as to clear the suit while East still has an entry.

In his textbook, East may have been given a sixth spade. The Rabbit couldn't be sure, but they were all very little spades, anyway, so it couldn't really matter whether there were five or six of them. The point of the hand was clear.

The Rabbit made a mental note to look it up when he got home. Meanwhile he carefully played the ♠7.

Papa's eyes clouded. If trumps broke 2-2, there should be no serious problem but what if they split 3-1? How could he avoid losing two trumps and two clubs? Had R.R. gone up with the ♠K, as any sane East would have done, all would have been plain sailing. After one round of trumps, Papa would have cashed the ♠A and discarded two clubs from dummy on his ♠QJ. Even if the third spade were ruffed, the contract would be safe.

Now it was much more difficult. Before long, however, the resourceful Greek had a plan.

He would lay down his two red aces, cross to dummy, first with the ♠A, then by trumping a spade, and ruff two diamonds on the way back. While this elimination was in progress, the ♣A would be cashed unobtrusively setting the stage for a brilliant endplay. If West started with ♣Kx and the desired shape, 3-1-7-2, he would be thrown in with the ♣K and forced to lead a diamond. Dummy's third club would disappear, while Papa ruffed with his last baby trump, and all would be well.

Of course, that was asking a lot of life: but then when a contract appeared unmakeable, the master prayed for the ideal distribution and brought off, if his prayers were granted, the seemingly impossible.

After going through the motions in his mind to make sure that his imaginative play wouldn't endanger the contract, if after all, trumps broke 2-2, Papa began the elimination.

When he came to the first diamond ruff, the Rueful Rabbit looked puzzled.

'It's my king of diamonds.' he said, after checking the cards carefully.

'And my trump,' retorted Papa.

'Trump?' repeated R.R., incredulously. 'A heart? But hearts aren't on the right. I mean, it's usual, er...,'

'It's usual,' broke in the Walrus irritably, 'to concentrate long enough to remember the contract, at least until trick one. We happen to be in four hearts.'

'I am sorry,' the Rabbit was crestfallen. 'Of course, had I known, that is, had I realized, I would have gone up with the king of spades. It's notrump in the textbooks, you know.

'All the same,' he went on reproachfully, 'it's really very confusing. It's all very well to play falsecards and things, because one is prepared for it. But when they start putting notrump on the right, as well, one can't help getting muddled. I mean...'

The distribution was almost right for Papa's plan, but not quite. The clubs were 3-3 and there was no way of avoiding defeat.

'Curious hand,' observed the Owl. 'The only way to defeat four hearts is to defend against three notrump. Most unusual.'

16. The Hog's Etiquette

The Ethics and Etiquette Committee of the Griffins Club held an emergency session on Friday to consider two charges of improper conduct against the Hideous Hog. The first was brought by Papa the Greek, who put forward this hand as evidence:

East-West Vul.
Dealer East

```
                    ♠ 6
                    ♡ J 9 8 7 3
                    ◇ 5 2
                    ♣ 9 8 7 6 2
  ♠ 5 3                          ♠ 10 9 8
  ♡ A K 2          N             ♡ Q 10 4
  ◇ K Q J 10 8 6  W   E          ◇ A 9 7
  ♣ 5 4              S            ♣ A K Q J
                    ♠ A K Q J 7 4 2
                    ♡ 6 5
                    ◇ 4 3
                    ♣ 10 3
```

West	North	East	South
Papa	R.R.	Karapet	H.H.
		1NT	2♡
3NT	pass	pass	dbl
redbl	all pass		

It wasn't in dispute that the Rueful Rabbit, sitting North, paused, squirmed and gulped uncomfortably, before passing over Papa's bid of 3NT. Neither was it in contention that the Hog, one of the fastest players and bidders in the country, went into a prolonged huddle, studied the ceiling and sighed deeply, before doubling.

'R.R.'s pause,' declared Papa presenting his case, 'was understandable. As ethical a player as you will find anywhere, he had a real problem — whether or not to sacrifice, bearing in mind the favorable vulnerability.

'But what reason was there for the long, pained trance preceding the Hog's double? Having psyched — and I confess that it took my poor partner in completely — he was determined to prevent the Rabbit from removing the double. And wherefore should he expect him to do that? Because of the Rabbit's long, unhappy pause over my three notrump, of course. Not only did H.H. take advantage of his partner's pause, in itself a highly improper thing to do,' pursued Papa, 'but he now resorted to a low and cynical maneuver. To stop R.R. from making the bid he feared, H.H. went into a spurious trance, sighing and grimacing, to create a false impression of uncertainty and doubt. He was telling the world that he had decided, though only just, on the closest of doubles. Of course, no ethical partner could remove it. H.H. might as well have bid deliberately out of turn.'

Putting down a gold-tipped, cigarette and lighting another, the Greek sat down with the air of a good man fighting evil.

Baring his teeth at the platform, in what was doubtless intended as a smile, the Hog began in a low key. 'It is never pleasant to concede a 1600 penalty,' were his opening words. 'To be outwitted, not to say humiliated by a better player must be galling. I can feel for Papa and therefore I forgive his bitterness. But,' added the Hog, in a voice vibrating with emotion, 'I repudiate entirely his unworthy suggestions.'

'Yes,' went on H.H., 'the Rabbit dithered for quite a time over Papa's three notrump and we now know, having seen his hand, that he might have been contemplating a sacrifice. He was just as likely, however, to be wondering where he had left his car or why his astrologer's predictions were so much more accurate about yesterday's events than about those of tomorrow. How can anyone tell what the Rabbit is thinking about when he has no idea himself?

'Of course,' pursued H.H., 'I drew no conclusions from his trance and paid no attention to it whatsoever.'

The Hog paused for dramatic effect. 'Alternatively,' he resumed and there was now a note of indignation in his voice, 'I had a duty to protect my, er, slightly unstable partner. He had shown unmistakably an urge to sacrifice in four hearts, and just as I knew it, so did Themistocles. What's more, he knew that I knew that he knew. But, knowing Papa, I knew something else too, from bitter experience. To intimidate the Rabbit he would redouble in a voice of thunder, which is, of course, precisely what he did. If R.R. thought of bidding four hearts before, he would surely do so now. Somehow I had to save him from himself.

'So you see, gentlemen,' declared H.H., 'either I wasn't influenced by R.R.'s pause or else I was protecting him against a predictable piece of sharp practice. Is it improper to guard against impropriety? Can it be wrong to prevent a wrong?' concluded H.H. rhetorically.

'I wonder how many wrongs make a right?' murmered Oscar the Owl, President of our Committee.

Judgment was deferred.

A Dialectic Squeeze

The second charge against H.H. brought forward jointly by Charlie the Chimp and Walter the Walrus, was that he had exceeded his rights as dummy, directed declarer, and engineered what was described in the indictment as a 'squeeze by dialectics'.

This was the deal which gave rise to the accusation:

North-South Vul.
Dealer West

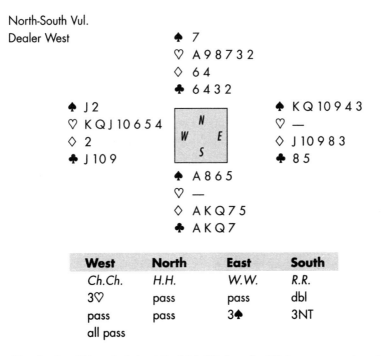

	♠ 7		
	♡ A 9 8 7 3 2		
	◊ 6 4		
	♣ 6 4 3 2		

♠ J 2		♠ K Q 10 9 4 3
♡ K Q J 10 6 5 4		♡ —
◊ 2		◊ J 10 9 8 3
♣ J 10 9		♣ 8 5

	♠ A 8 6 5	
	♡ —	
	◊ A K Q 7 5	
	♣ A K Q 7	

West	North	East	South
Ch.Ch.	H.H.	W.W.	R.R.
3♡	pass	pass	dbl
pass	pass	3♠	3NT
all pass			

Charlie the Chimp led the ♠J which Walter the Walrus overtook to lead another spade, followed by a third one. The Rabbit played low twice.

Then he went up with the ♠A and tabled his hand. 'I'll save time,' he announced, 'and just take my nine tricks.'

'Which nine tricks?' demanded the Chimp, the Walrus and two kibitzers in unison.

'Why the ace of spades of course,' replied the Rabbit, 'the ace of hearts, four clubs and...'

'How do you get at the ace of hearts?' inquired the Chimp.

'Who said that the clubs broke 3-2?' asked the Walrus.

'If they don't I, er, well, I mean...' dithered the Rabbit.

'As it happens, the clubs break nicely for you' broke in the Chimp, showing his ♣J109, 'but you couldn't claim more than three tricks before testing them. Four clubs, however, only give you eight tricks.'

'One down,' declared the Walrus, inscribing 100 above the line in his 'We' column.

The Hog who had been strangely quiescent, now came to life and addressed the Rabbit in a soft, silky voice.

'You are quite right, R.R., to save time. It's later than you think, you know,' he added, turning to the Walrus and the Chimp. 'But since there seems to be some doubt about it, perhaps it would be best to play the hand out the kindergarten way. You start, no doubt, with the ace of diamonds and...'

'Who said so?' demanded the Chimp suspiciously.

'You have to play something,' retorted the Hog, 'and it's only natural to begin with the best suit. Besides, if you show out in diamonds, the clubs can't break, so the hand's a spread.'

'Are you suggesting,' asked the Walrus, who didn't like to be trifled with, 'that you are more likely to make nine tricks if clubs yield three tricks than if they yield four?'

'You make nine tricks anyway,' replied the H.H., 'but it's easier if the clubs break badly.'

'But I have a diamond and clubs break nicely,' broke in the Chimp. 'So take your ace of diamonds, four clubs...'

'Only three clubs,' insisted the Hog.

'Then you're two down,' cried W.W., angrily, inscribing another 100 in his 'We' column.

'Presumably,' went on the Hog, ignoring him, 'you will lay down the ace and king of clubs, and seeing all follow, continue with the seven.'

'Why?' asked the Chimp.

'He need do no such thing,' protested the Walrus, suspicious of the Hog on principle.

'If he doesn't he'll make four clubs and it's been agreed that we claim only three,' countered H.H. 'You've even taken another 100 for it, Walter, so you can hardly object.'

'Besides,' went on H.H., 'declarer is bound by his statement. He has claimed the ace of hearts and how else can he get to it if Charlie doesn't lead a heart, and how can he lead one if he doesn't come on play? He must be presented with a club or his hand is dead.'

The Walrus growled uneasily. Some hanky-panky was afoot, but for the life of him he couldn't see the catch.

The Rabbit, confused by a conversation he couldn't follow, brightened visibly. 'I don't know whether it's better to take three clubs or four, but I really can't see why I shouldn't make the ace of hearts. After all, it's my dummy.'

Breathing heavily, he laid down the ♣A, then the ♣K, and after hovering nervously over the ♣Q, he finally extracted the ♣7.

With only hearts left, Charlie the Chimp led the ♡K.

The Rabbit's fingers stretched automatically for the ♡A, but the Hog promptly stopped him.

'No, no,' he warned him, 'that wouldn't be in accordance with your statement. You've claimed nine tricks specifically, not ten and you've only lost three so far. You must concede another. Otherwise, if the diamonds break...'

'They do nothing of the sort,' roared the Walrus, 'I had five and I've four left so even if you've exchanged a club trick for a heart, you're still one down.'

The Hog nodded sympathetically. 'Quite so,' he agreed, 'but declarer isn't entitled to know about all those diamonds of yours and he mustn't risk making an overtrick. So he lets the king of hearts hold, wins the next heart and claims.'

'Claims? Claims what?' bellowed the Walrus.

'His contract of course,' rejoined the Hog. 'He has thrown a diamond and the queen of clubs on those two hearts, and before leaving dummy, cashes the six of clubs. You will allow him, I hope, to score three of his four club tricks. At this point, three spades, two hearts, one diamond and four clubs will have been played, and as you follow to that club, the position will be:

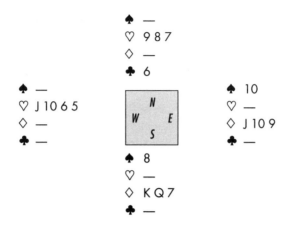

```
              ♠ —
              ♡ 9 8 7
              ◇ —
              ♣ 6
♠ —                          ♠ 10
♡ J 10 6 5      N            ♡ —
◇ —          W     E         ◇ J 10 9
♣ —             S            ♣ —
              ♠ 8
              ♡ —
              ◇ K Q 7
              ♣ —
```

The Rabbit went through the motions. The Walrus detached one card, then another, before, spluttering with rage, he finally let go a diamond allowing the ◇7 to yield the Rabbit his ninth trick.

'It was a mistake to throw the diamond,' remarked a junior kibitzer, only recently promoted from watching the backgammon.

'We've been conned!' cried the outraged Walrus.

'Bamboozled! Cheated!' echoed the Chimp. 'He had no right to make all those insidious suggestions.'

'I was only trying to save time,' explained the Hog, winking impishly at the spectators who had gathered around the table.

'Excuse me, sir,' asked a serious-minded kibitzer, 'but I didn't quite follow your remark about the ace of diamonds at trick four. You said that if West showed out, the clubs must be 4-1 and declarer could claim. Why would you...?'

'Oh, a Madeira, I think. Very kind of you.' The Hog was ready with the right answer. 'That ace of diamonds now. Well, West has no diamonds, only two spades and seven hearts — he can't have more, for there are six in dummy — he must have four clubs. We no longer have to create a loser but simply play out the clubs, bringing about the position you've just seen. The only difference is that the squeeze card will be the ace of hearts instead of the fourth club.'

'And what if East, not West has four clubs?' persisted the kibitzer.

'That makes it easier than ever,' replied the Hog. 'If West has three black cards only, he must have three diamonds, so diamonds break 3-3 and declarer has one spade, five diamonds and three clubs. He can't go wrong.'

'Not played by dummy,' observed another kibitzer, joining in the conversation. 'Now if the hand were played by declarer...'

17. The Age of Chivalry

The old year ended on a happy note for the Hideous Hog, full of promise for the days ahead.

Bidding partner's hand has always been a basic tenet of the Hog philosophy and no one has ever accused him of failing to practice what he preaches. Playing partner's cards is more difficult, technically, but the Hog has been mastering the art and he has scored lately some notable successes.

'One day,' he told us over a friendly magnum at the Griffins New Year's Party, 'I may be able to eliminate partner altogether. He will just sit there like a zombie, carrying out my orders, without bidding or playing anything on his own initiative. Yes, I have great faith in the future.'

'But why shouldn't partner play, too' protested Oscar the Owl, our Senior Kibitzer. 'He pays table money, buys you drinks, surely he has a right...'

'A right?' broke in H.H. indignantly. 'You may as well say that a lunatic has a right to set his house on fire so long as he pays the mortgage. What if you live in the same house? And how about helpless old ladies crossing roads? Have they, too, the right to get run over or should you take control and guide them through the traffic?'

'One has moral obligations in life,' went on the Hog warmly, 'and though partner may have the right, as you say, to play and bid on his own and to commit suicide, it is your duty to stop him doing it as long as possible or till the end of the rubber anyway.'

Two recent deals had given the Hog full scope to discharge his lofty moral obligations. This was one of them:

Neither Vul.
Dealer East

```
                    ♠ 6 5 4 2
                    ♡ 9 6 3
                    ◇ A 9 6 5
                    ♣ A J
    ♠ 8 3
    ♡ 5 4 2            N
    ◇ J 2         W        E
    ♣ 7 6 5 4 3 2     S
```

West	North	East	South
H.H.	D.S.	W.W.	Papa
		1♡	1♠
pass	2♣	pass	3♠
pass	4♠	pass	pass
dbl	all pass		

'I was West, as you have doubtless guessed,' pursued the Hog. 'My usual sort of hand. Papa, also as usual, had enough to reach game. A straightforward bidding sequence...'

'Particularly the double,' chipped in Colin the Corgi, the facetious young man from Oxbridge.

The Hog turned on him quickly. 'A defender's first duty,' he declared, jerking imperiously a fat pink forefinger, 'is to do nothing to help declarer. Can you seriously contend that my double would do that? Of course not. And it's safe. After such hesitant bidding no one can redouble and an overtrick is unlikely. Besides, how did I know that the Walrus shouldn't have doubled himself? Somebody had to bid his cards.'

We went through the play. The Hog opened a heart to W.W.'s king and ace, Papa shedding the queen and jack. Ruffing a third heart, the Greek proceeded with the ♣K, a club to dummy's ace and a trump on which Walter played the queen. Papa won the trick with the ace and continued with the jack of trumps.

'Well,' said the Hog when he had reached this point in the story, 'have you beaten the contract?'

C.C. hooted noncommittally. P.P. tried to look inscrutable.

'I followed suit conscientiously all the way,' said C.C. 'but you, no doubt, thought of something even better.'

'Certainly' declared H.H., 'and if it will assist you in any way, I can tell you now that Walter won the third trick for our side with the king of spades.'

Oscar the Owl looked sorely puzzled. 'Do you mean,' he asked 'that with those tram tickets you somehow stopped declarer...'

'No, no,' interrupted the Hog, 'I wasn't concerned with declarer. Needless to say, he couldn't make the contract on his own, but I had to stop Walter presenting him with it, which, left to himself he would have done with alacrity. You see it all, don't you?' asked H.H. fixing the Toucan with a malevolent look.

'Yes, er, yes,' replied T.T. bouncing unsteadily.

'Then I'd better explain,' went on the Hog. 'Papa's hand was an open book. He started with two hearts. We know that for he followed twice. He could hardly have a third club or he would have ruffed it. Spades? With six to the ace-king he would have laid down the ace before touching clubs, so I could tell from his play that he had five trumps, missing two honours which is why he wanted to lead trumps from dummy.'

'Elementary,' cooed Colin softly.

'Precisely,' agreed H.H. 'so elementary, in fact, that even the Walrus was bound to see it. That was the danger. Knowing that declarer had no hearts or clubs left, he would be careful not to present him with a ruff and discard. He would lead a diamond — and present him instead with his unmakeable contract. You may as well see the full deal: the Hog filled in the other hands.

```
              ♠ 6 5 4 2
              ♡ 9 6 3
              ◇ A 9 6 5
              ♣ A J
  ♠ 8 3                          ♠ K Q
  ♡ 5 4 2          N             ♡ A K 10 8 7
  ◇ J 2       W         E        ◇ Q 4 3
  ♣ 7 6 5 4 3 2      S           ♣ Q 10 9
              ♠ A J 10 9 7
              ♡ Q J
              ◇ K 10 8 7
              ♣ K 8
```

'I couldn't be sure of the diamond position,' continued H.H., 'but it was crystal clear that if Papa didn't have the king of diamonds, he would lose the contract anyway and if he had both the king and queen he couldn't fail to make it. So I was concerned only with the actual distribution, as you see it, and my object was to prevent Walter from leading a diamond. Any ideas?'

After a brief pause to make sure that the magnum was empty, H.H. resumed. 'Fortunately, that Walrus is eminently bamboozalable, for though he knows precious little about bridge, he knows all about points, conventions, echoes, and signals of every sort. So all I had to do was to play the eight of spades before the three, proclaiming three trumps and a desire to ruff. Seeing the eight, even Walter could work out that my third trump, the one I didn't have, was the nine. Thereupon he duly led a heart. The ruff and discard was, of course, useless to Papa, who still had to concede a diamond.'

'So the helpless old lady was escorted safely across the road' observed Oscar the Owl.

'Chivalrous, as always,' remarked the Corgi. H.H. didn't hear him. He was busy scribbling.

PROMOTING A LOSER

'Here you are,' he announced. 'You can look at all four hands and play double-dummy if you like. And talking of helpless old ladies, you may as well know that my partner was that Rabbit, the luckiest player in the universe. Why, he cuts me three times out of four and when you are at the receiving end, believe me, it feels like four times out of three. He tries to make up for it, mind you, by holding good cards, but then that's the least a poor player can do.'

Neither Vul
Dealer South
North-South 30 on

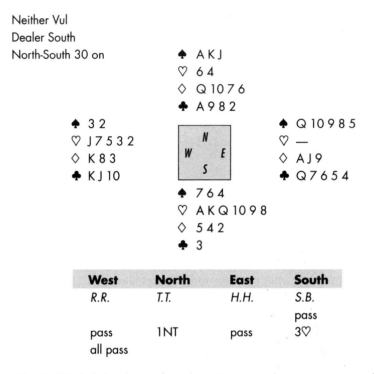

♠ A K J
♡ 6 4
◊ Q 10 7 6
♣ A 9 8 2

♠ 3 2
♡ J 7 5 3 2
◊ K 8 3
♣ K J 10

♠ Q 10 9 8 5
♡ —
◊ A J 9
♣ Q 7 6 5 4

♠ 7 6 4
♡ A K Q 10 9 8
◊ 5 4 2
♣ 3

West	North	East	South
R.R.	T.T.	H.H.	S.B.
			pass
pass	1NT	pass	3♡
all pass			

'The Rabbit led the three of spades. Sizing up the situation at a glance, the Secretary Bird went up with dummy's ace and confidently led a trump to his queen. When I showed out he went into a huddle, crossed his long, spindly legs, hissed, murmured darkly about murdering someone in his past incarnation and looked at the ceiling for inspiration.

'Eventually he led a club to the ace, ruffed a club with the eight in the closed hand and went over to dummy with a spade to the king.'

The Hog paused.

'A very good hand,' said the Corgi 'and now shall I show you a slam I...'

Dismissing the offer with a short, contemptuous snarl, H.H. resumed:

'Naturally, I could tell every card. Declarer's hearts were so good that he couldn't have another picture or he wouldn't have passed as dealer. He started off jauntily, because he thought he could see nine tricks. Dummy had three, so he was relying on six trump tricks. He ruffed the second club with the eight, presumably his lowest trump, and he won trick two with the queen of hearts, so his trump holding had to be exactly what it was. I could place every pip. You can see, of course, what was going to happen.'

As he looked for an un-empty glass, the Hog waited for a helpful question.

'That slam I was going to tell you about,' began the Corgi. 'I had the king to...'

This time the Hideous Hog didn't even trouble to snarl.

'Declarer,' he continued hastily, 'would ruff another club and exit with his third spade. The Rabbit, who led the three, followed on the second round with the deuce, so there was no mystery about that suit. But what would R.R. play on the third spade? He would have at this stage four trumps and three diamonds, so he would, of course, throw a diamond and it would be all over. He would be endplayed in trumps. S.B. would have three losing diamonds as before, but the Rabbit with trumps only left, would eventually have to ruff my ace of diamonds and lead a trump into the AK10.'

'Unless you save her quickly from the oncoming bus, the helpless old lady will be run over,' warned the Owl.

'Exactly' agreed the Hog. 'The Rabbit had to be made to shorten his trumps before it was too late. To be more precise, I had to compel him to ruff that third spade and the only way I could do it was by throwing my queen under the king so as to promote the jack.'

The Hog paused but seeing C.C. open his mouth, he went on quickly. 'Luckily, that Rabbit has learned to observe the fall of the honor cards, some of the time anyway, and he spotted my queen. He concluded no doubt, that I had a doubleton and that declarer had been dealt sixteen cards. That sort of thing never bothers R.R. So, when declarer ruffed a club and played a spade, he ruffed and led a low diamond to my jack. I returned the nine of diamonds to his king and was on play at the decisive moment with the ace of diamonds. Having nothing but trumps left, the Rabbit couldn't even revoke and his jack won the setting trick. You see,' concluded the Hog, 'how carefully I had to play his cards to break the contract.'

'I felt all along' observed the Corgi with a sigh 'that H.H. would contrive to rescue that helpless old lady. The age of chivalry...'

18. Satanic Hands

'The Devil's getting old,' scoffed the Hideous Hog. 'He's not what he used to be in my young days. As for his girlfriends...' A deprecatory gesture rounded off the sentence.

We were discussing the strange events of the night before, Walpurgis, when according to ancient lore, the witches ride out on broomsticks for a tryst with their master, the Devil.

April 30th is by tradition gala night at the Griffins. The Witches' Sabbath always presents a challenge, bringing with it a sense of danger and excitement. As night falls and the cards dance to the Devil's tune there's a shock for someone on every deal. And so it was this time.

The centerpiece was a deal starring Walter the Walrus, the club's premier exponent of the point-count. A retired accountant from earliest youth, the Walrus is dedicated to figures and firmly believes that it is more honorable to go down with points to spare than to bring home a flimsy contract on suspect values. As he sorted his hand, there was a flash of lightning in the still night sky, then peals of thunder, drawing nearer and nearer. With Oscar the Owl, our Senior Kibitzer, I sat down between the Hog and the Walrus, who picked up:

♠ Q 10 9
♡ K J
♢ K Q
♣ A K Q J 10 9

I was wondering whether, after opening 2♣, he would rebid 3♣ or 3NT, when the Rueful Rabbit, who dealt as West, put an end to all speculations by opening 1♠.

West	North	East	South
R.R.	T.T.	H.H.	W.W.
1♠	pass	1NT	dbl
2♡	pass	pass	2NT
pass	pass	dbl	all pass

Fearing, no doubt that his opponents might have a cheap save in hearts, the Walrus cautiously refrained from redoubling. Why paint the lily?

Rightly interpreting the double as a command for a spade lead, the Rabbit played the ♠6 to the ♠K. The ♡10 came back. This was the deal in full.

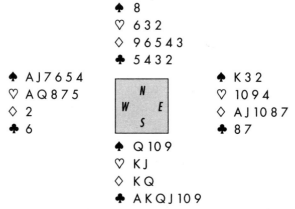

```
              ♠ 8
              ♡ 6 3 2
              ◊ 9 6 5 4 3
              ♣ 5 4 3 2
♠ A J 7 6 5 4                    ♠ K 3 2
♡ A Q 8 7 5        N             ♡ 10 9 4
◊ 2            W       E         ◊ A J 10 8 7
♣ 6                S             ♣ 8 7
              ♠ Q 10 9
              ♡ K J
              ◊ K Q
              ♣ A K Q J 10 9
```

After the two top hearts the Rabbit played a third one to the Hog's ♡9. A spade came back, followed by an avalanche of spades and hearts. When the last one glided across the green baize the Walrus remained with three cards — the ◊KQ and the ♣A. Which should he throw?

After detaching and replacing each one in turn, he finally let go the ♣A and much to his surprise R.R. scored the penultimate trick with the ♣6. The ◊A followed.

'Curious hand,' observed O.O., 'the only card in the club suit to win a trick was the six.'

An owl hooted jubilantly from a tree in the garden.

The Walrus was spluttering indignantly. 'I had twenty-one points to their nineteen. They made thirteen tricks, I made none. I am no egalitarian, but such flagrant injustice is an affront to the laws of the universe.'

19. The Rabbit Discards the Queen of Trumps

Molly the Mule, star of the Mermaids, paid us another visit on Thursday, this month's Ladies Day. Her first partner was the Emeritus Professor of Bio-Sophistry, known on account of his habits and appearance as the Secretary Bird. Pitted against them were the Rueful Rabbit and Walter the Walrus.

The Hideous Hog, too late to cut in, was kibitzing for the house, as he put it, which meant that on every deal his sympathies were with declarer. It was in the public interest, he explained, to raise the standard of the game, so the sooner he got into it, the better for all concerned.

As I walked over to join them, I heard Charlie the Chimp, who was kibitzing against the Professor, say to the Rabbit:

'You should have bid three notrump. Then no one could ruff...'

'One club,' called the Walrus.

'Pass,' said Molly.

'With five spades I thought it would be safer...' began R.R.

'It's your bid,' bellowed the Walrus.

Neither Vul.
Dealer North

```
                        ♠ A 7 5
                        ♡ A K Q
                        ◇ Q 7 4
                        ♣ 10 9 8 3
   ♠ K 6 4 2                              ♠ 3
   ♡ 9 8 7              ┌─────────┐       ♡ 6 5 4 3 2
   ◇ A K 2           W  │    N    │  E    ◇ 10 8 6 5
   ♣ J 6 2              │    S    │       ♣ A 7 5
                        └─────────┘
                        ♠ Q J 10 9 8
                        ♡ J 10
                        ◇ J 9 3
                        ♣ K Q 4
```

West	**North**	**East**	**South**
S.B.	W.W.	M.M.	R.R.
	1♣	pass	1♠
pass	1NT	pass	2NT
pass	3♠	pass	4♠
all pass			

While S.B. considered his lead, R.R. resumed his dialog with the Chimp.
'I am all for notrump as you know, but on a diamond lead...'

'At the Mermaids,' said Molly severely, 'we never discuss the previous hand.'

'It's not the previous hand,' corrected the Rabbit, setting the record straight, 'it is the one before when you ruffed my king of spades and...'

The Professor led the ◇K, then the ◇A. Next he switched to a heart.

'Unlucky hand,' whispered Oscar the Owl, our Senior Kibitzer, to one of his juniors. 'Declarer has three top losers and though the king of spades is under the ace, it's too well guarded to be caught.'

At trick four the Rabbit led the ♣3 from dummy. Molly played low and the king won. The ♠Q held the next trick and the ♠J the one after, Molly discarding a heart. The Rabbit counted his tricks carefully. There were eight certainties — three spades, three hearts, the ◇Q and one club, which he had scored already. A second club would bring the total to nine. Yes, the Chimp was right: it was a lot easier in notrump, having to make nine tricks instead of ten.

He went on by cashing the ♡K, then the ♡A on which he played the ♠8 from his hand. With six tricks stacked neatly in front of him, the Rabbit stretched out for the ♣10.

'You're in your hand,' called out the Walrus. 'Your hand,' snapped Molly.

'But the ace of hearts,' protested the Rabbit. 'I mean, that is…'

'No doubt on some other deal you were in dummy,' hissed the Professor 'but on this one you happen to be in your hand, so if it's not too much trouble would you kindly detach a card and place it on the table.'

The Rabbit felt sure he was right, but being in a minority of one there was nothing he could do. Bitterly, he regretted cashing that third heart, for now he had to lead a club from dummy and, whether he crossed over with a spade or a diamond, he would be setting up another winner for the defense.

With an inward sigh he led a diamond to dummy's queen, then the ♣10. Molly played low nonchalantly, but the Rabbit rose with the queen, while the Secretary Bird cunningly dropped the jack.

At that the Rabbit s spirits rose. Not only had he nine tricks, but there was now the faint hope of a tenth without risk, for if Molly had two clubs left she could only have one red card.

So, reflected the Rabbit, other things weren't quite equal. If he cashed the ♠A he couldn't possibly come to another trick. With a club there was a slight chance. One could never tell.

When the Rabbit exited with his ♣4, this was the position:

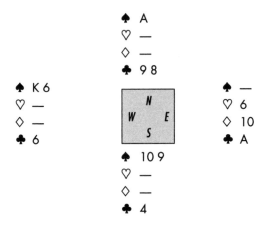

The Secretary Bird

Molly returned the ◊10 and the Secretary Bird, with a dangerous gleam in his pince-nez, played the spade king on R.R.'s ten.

The Rabbit screwed his eyes as he tried to concentrate. Molly's last card ought to be a club and yet he had an uneasy feeling that the Professor, who shouldn't have had a club, had followed to the previous trick. One thing, however, was certain. Molly couldn't have a spade, so obviously the ace was right discard.

The wild tufts of hair over S.B.'s ears bristled angrily.

'Why did you smother me?' he cried in anguish. 'All you had to do was to go up with your ace of clubs and lead another.'

'How was I to know,' countered Molly, 'that you had the king of spades? Had you refrained from cashing your top diamonds you would have had a chance to knock out the ace of spades. Just like a man to make a mistake and blame a woman.'

The Hog smiled contentedly. He enjoyed a little ill feeling and the contract had been made so it hadn't been a waste of time.

'Curious coincidence.' observed the Hog to the Owl. 'The Rabbit finds the only way to lose three notrump, which he believes to be the contract, and that's the only way to make four spades, which actually is.'

A Case for Intuition

Still dazed, wondering what had hit him, or rather what he had done unwittingly to hit others, the Rabbit heard Molly open 3◊ on the next hand.

North-South Vul.
Dealer East

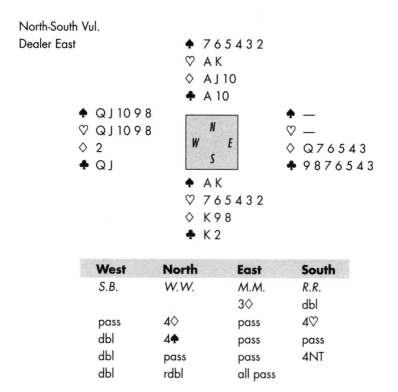

```
                  ♠ 7 6 5 4 3 2
                  ♡ A K
                  ◊ A J 10
                  ♣ A 10
♠ Q J 10 9 8                          ♠ —
♡ Q J 10 9 8         N               ♡ —
◊ 2            W         E            ◊ Q 7 6 5 4 3
♣ Q J               S                ♣ 9 8 7 6 5 4 3
                  ♠ A K
                  ♡ 7 6 5 4 3 2
                  ◊ K 9 8
                  ♣ K 2
```

West	North	East	South
S.B.	W.W.	M.M.	R.R.
		3◊	dbl
pass	4◊	pass	4♡
dbl	4♠	pass	pass
dbl	pass	pass	4NT
dbl	rdbl	all pass	

The Walrus was outraged. After a preemptive bid he could visualize a freakish distribution with bad breaks in both majors, but he could see enough high-card points to be in the slam zone and Walter the Walrus was the last man to allow anyone to trifle with his points. The redouble was, so to speak, a point of honor.

The Professor fingered the ♣Q, then the ♡Q.

'Whichever he leads,' said O.O., *sotto voce*, 'declarer has enough entries to set up the suit and wrap up ten tricks.'

After due deliberation the Professor led the ◊2.

The Rabbit inserted dummy's jack, and while Molly detached the ◊3, then the ◊7, and replacing both sat back to think again, R.R.

counted his tricks. Seeing nine, he brightened visibly, for that meant that he would only go one down.

With a sigh of relief he played the ◊8 from his hand. As it touched the table his heart massed a beat, then another, for he realized a fraction of a second too late that Molly had covered the jack with the queen. Now the penalty would be 1000.

Suppressing an inward gurgle and wiping the beads of perspiration from his forehead, the Rabbit tried to look unconcerned.

Molly frowned, asked to see the trick again and returned the ♣9.

It didn't seem to matter in which order he cashed his eight tricks, but hoping to conceal his gaffe he went through the motions slowly and with deliberation.

Winning the trick with dummy's ♣A, he came back to his hand with the ♣K and continued with the ◊9. For some reason which R.R. couldn't fathom, S.B. went into a trance. Eventually, with marked reluctance, he threw a heart. The Rabbit won with the ◊A, cashed the ♡A and ♡K and returned to the closed hand with the ◊K on which the Secretary Bird discarded a spade.

It began to dawn on the Rabbit that S.B. had no clubs left and it was therefore safe for him to play a third round of hearts. The Professor returned a spade and now another heart set up two winners in the suit with the ♠A as an entry. A moment later the Rabbit had ten tricks and no one even noticed his *faux pas* at trick one.

'Why didn't you throw a spade instead of that catastrophic heart on the second round of diamonds?' cried Molly.

'Because had I done so,' retorted the Secretary Bird with a vicious, rasping sound in his throat, 'the trick would be won with the ten of diamonds, not the ace, and after cashing the ace and king of spades declarer would still have three entries in dummy — the ace of diamonds and the ace and king of hearts — to set up and enjoy the spades. Now had you only returned a second diamond, I would have thrown a club and there would have been no squeeze.'

'And that's just what I wanted to do,' declared Molly. 'I had a feeling, an intuition, and my intuitions never let me down. But when my queen held the trick how could I help placing you with the king and R.R. with a singleton?'

'Couldn't the contract still be made?' asked the Hog softly. The kibitzers looked up for there was a strange diffidence in his manner.

'Of course not,' said Molly the Mule.

'Obviously,' echoed the Professor.

'I wonder,' said H.H. hesitantly. 'Feminine intuition has been known to be wrong.'

'Not mine,' rejoined Molly.

'Champagne?' cooed the Hog.

'Certainly,' replied Molly.

The Hog reflected. What was one case to a woman whose husband was President of the International Consortium of Keyhole Manufacturers? Chickenfeed.

'Would you care to make it two cases?' he went on in his silkiest voice.

'No,' replied Molly firmly. 'I do not bet professionally — unlike some people,' she added with a meaning look.

'Very well then,' said the Hog, 'but tell them not to deliver it before eleven o'clock. I need plenty of sleep in this weather.' All trace of humility had gone from his voice.

'Your intuition tells you to return another diamond at trick two?' asked the Hog.

'Of course, and the Professor parts with a club,' replied Molly.

'I win with the ace of diamonds and return to my hand with the king of diamonds,' said H.H.

'The professor throws his second club. Now what?' asked Molly defiantly.

'I continue with the two of clubs, and the Professor...' The Hog left the sentence unfinished.

'A heart,' said Molly.

'Then,' went on the Hog, 'I win with the ace of clubs, cash the ace and king of hearts and get back with the king of clubs to play a third round of hearts. That leaves S.B. with one heart only and I remain with the ace and king of spades, allowing me to set up two long hearts as R.R. did just now.'

'You rushed me, giving me no time to think,' protested Molly. 'On that two of clubs the Professor threw a spade of course, not a heart.'

'Then I would win with the ten of diamonds,' said H.H., 'cash the ace and king of spades and still have three entries in dummy — the ace of clubs and the ace and king of hearts — to set up and enjoy the spades.'

Grinning at the kibitzers the Hog added, 'It was R.R.'s masculine intuition in letting you hold the first trick that won the day, you know. After that master-stroke the contract was unbeatable.'

'Male chauvinist Hog,' said Molly scornfully, rising from the table.

20. Monster Math

'Are you sure?' asked the Hog anxiously.

'Positive,' replied Oscar the Owl. 'I have it from the Walrus himself.'

'In that case,' said H.H., rising from the table, 'I will double my wager before it's too late. So if you'll excuse me, while you order drinks, I'll call up my bookmakers.'

We were chatting about the prospects in the annual match between the Friends of Bacchus and the Old Boys of St. Swithin's, which was to be played that evening. The news that had sent the Hog scurrying to the telephone was that starring for the Old Boys would be W.W.'s younger brother, Sylvester, Senior Statistician at St. Swithin's.

Sylvester shared his elder brother's keen interest in figures and was as dedicated to percentages and probabilities as the Walrus was to the point count. The Hog had only met him once, but he had heard him expound his philosophy of bridge and that was enough.

'Basically, it's an easy game,' Sylvester had assured us over a decanter of Taylor '63. 'You need a modicum of technique, of course,' he waved that aside, 'but thereafter it's purely a question of figures. In every situation one chance is superior to others. The key to success lies in knowing which it is, in other words, in correctly computing the odds.

'Tables and formulae are of help,' went on S.S., 'and a few dozen should be memorized, but the born mathematician doesn't really need them. He can work out the probabilities as they arise.'

The Hog's only comment was an eloquent snort. It was beneath his dignity to vouchsafe a considered reply but he took the subject up next day over a glass of madeira at the Griffins bar.

'Give me the facts and you can keep the figures,' he told us. 'All the twice-two-make-four mystique isn't for me.'

'But if twice two don't make four,' protested the Toucan, 'what do they make?'

'That,' retorted the Hog, 'depends entirely on what you are adding and on who does the addition. On the lower plane of abstract, dehydrated numerals, I grant you two plus two equals four. By all means, bear it in mind when you buy peanuts, measure floorboards or build an apparatus to travel in outer space. But of what relevance are equations to the high side of life, to love, to poetry, to bridge?

'When I have two trumps in my hand and two more in dummy, does that come to four? Of course not. The total is more likely to be five, if not six, though it's barely three when the Rabbit has them.

'The human element,' concluded the Hog, 'will always make a monkey out of mathematics.'

Supporters of both sides gathered in strength to watch the annual encounter between the Friends of Bacchus, captained by H.H., and the Old Boys at St. Swithin's, led by their Senior Statistician. I settled down to watch the brothers.

In appearance they had little in common. Smaller, more compact than the Walrus, Sylvester's short, squat legs were surmounted by a long, rectilinear body, not unlike a well-filled cube. Appended to the thickset neck was a large head, somewhat reminiscent of an outsize electric light bulb and just as impersonal. Between the glistening bald dome and the small receding chin protruded a long, pointed nose. Opaque dark glasses obscured the rest of his features. Everything about Sylvester proclaimed the scientist and the academic. Among his major unpublished works, I was told, were *The Mathematical Key to the Universe* and its sequel *Simple Secrets of Creation*.

Sylvester sat South for St. Swithin's, the Hog for the Friends of Bacchus. This deal, which came up towards the end of the first half, provided a good test for their rival philosophies.

Neither Vul.
Dealer South

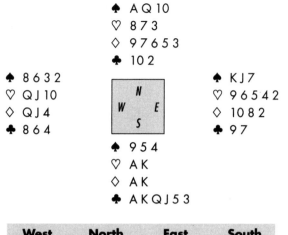

♠ A Q 10
♥ 8 7 3
◇ 9 7 6 5 3
♣ 10 2

♠ 8 6 3 2
♥ Q J 10
◇ Q J 4
♣ 8 6 4

♠ K J 7
♥ 9 6 5 4 2
◇ 10 8 2
♣ 9 7

♠ 9 5 4
♥ A K
◇ A K
♣ A K Q J 5 3

West	North	East	South
	W.W.		S.S.
			2♣
pass	2◇	pass	3NT
pass	4NT	pass	6NT
all pass			

The lead was the ♥Q to declarer's ace. S.S. began by reeling off his six clubs, throwing two diamonds and two hearts from dummy, and watching the discards intently. West shed three spades. East, keeping to the same pattern as dummy, threw four hearts.

With eleven tricks on top, Sylvester looked to the spades to provide the twelfth and his next move was a low spade to dummy's ten, losing to East's jack. Back on play with the ace of diamonds, he led another spade, all set to finesse the queen. When West showed out, he shrugged his shoulders philosophically.

'Bound to be the same result in the other room,' he said. 'No one can keep out of a slam on these holdings or make it as the cards lie.'

'Diamonds break 3-3,' chipped in an amateur kibitzer, sporting the champagne and burgundy tie of the Friends of Bacchus.

The mathematician turned on him with that air of lofty condescension which comes so naturally to academics.

'You are very observant,' he said, raising a sardonic eyebrow, 'but it so happens that there are three chances in four of finding West with one of the spade honors. The 3-3 diamond break will occur no more than 35.53 percent of the time. Ergo, the first line of play is superior to the second as 75 is to 35.53, the ratio being, as any child will tell you exactly...'

The amateur kibitzer retired abashed.

At half-time the Friends of Bacchus were leading by 1100, nearly all the points coming from this one hand on which H.H. getting the same opening, made the slam.

'How did he play it?' I asked Oscar, who had been kibitzing H.H.

'At trick two,' said O.O., 'he led the king of diamonds. Then, after pausing for nearly five seconds, he cashed the ace, crossed to the ten of clubs and led a third diamond. When the suit broke 3-3 there was no further problem.'

'Wasn't that an inferior play?' I asked H.H. when we had finished comparing scores. 'Surely, whatever the result, you should have taken two finesses in spades, giving yourself a seventy-five percent chance.'

'Not enough,' retorted the Hog. 'I like to make my own odds and here I have myself well over ninety percent.'

'But...' began Peregrine the Penguin joining in the discussion.

'Not at all,' retorted H.H. 'If the diamonds are not divided 3-3 I can still play on the spades, so you see, I can have my cake and eat it, too, and no logarithm-monger can do better than that.'

The Penguin looked up.

'Please don't always interrupt,' said the Hog severely. 'You are obviously wondering how I could tell whether or not the diamonds would split 3-3. The key, of course, was my play at trick two. You may recall that before touching the clubs or revealing anything about my hand, I laid down the king of diamonds. Now, since you are all so interested in probabilities, perhaps you can tell me how many defenders in our day and age would fail to give each other the count in this situation. Not one in ten, not one in twenty, if you play quickly enough.

'So,' concluded the Hog, 'when West followed with the four and East with the two. I had little doubt, that whatever your paper odds, the diamonds were 3-3. Not knowing what was afoot, the defenders were hardly likely to deceive each other with false signals.'

LOOKING FOR THE EXTRA CHANCE

During the second half the Old Boys gathered round their Senior Statistician, oozing moral support from every loyal pore. Sylvester knew that he was the man of the moment and he was ready to count and compute as he had never done before. Soon a deal came up made for his mathematical genius.

North-South Vul.
Dealer South

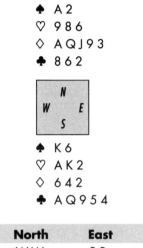

♠	A 2
♡	9 8 6
◇	A Q J 9 3
♣	8 6 2

♠	K 6
♡	A K 2
◇	6 4 2
♣	A Q 9 5 4

West	North	East	South
H.H.	W.W.	R.R.	S.S.
			1NT
pass	3NT	all pass	

The Hog opened the ♣7 to the Rabbit's ten. Sylvester won with the king and studied the situation in depth.

I could see what was running through his mind. If the diamond finesse was right or if the suit broke reasonably well, there was no problem. But what if East had five diamonds or four to the K10? Would the contract then be doomed?

The minutes ticked away as S.S. pondered. Then, having made up his mind, he suddenly swished the ♣A on the table, bringing down the king from the Hog.

An admiring gasp went up from the kibitzers.

The Senior Statistician's features, so taut and tense a moment before, relaxed into a triumphant smile.

'Forgive me, gentlemen,' he said, 'if I venture to comment briefly on my play, but you will agree, I think, that the situation is of unusual interest.'

No one said a word as S.S. explained how he had looked everywhere for an extra chance to guard against a bad diamond break. There existed one hope and one only, the bare king of clubs with West. Then a low club to dummy's eight would force out East's jack or ten and a simple finesse would pick up the other honor. With four club tricks in the bag, the diamond finesse would no longer be needed.

'Admittedly,' concluded S.S., 'finding a singleton king of clubs with West was only a 2.86 percent chance, but casinos the world over thrive on such slender odds, and as you've just seen, they can ensure success at bridge, too.'

The Hog coughed.

'Need I go through the motions?' asked the mathematician.

'Just for the record,' said H.H. amiably.

At trick three, Sylvester led a low club. The Hog waved playfully the club ten in mid-air, then dropped it on the table together with a spade.

This was the deal in full:

```
                    ♠ A 2
                    ♡ 9 8 6
                    ◇ A Q J 9 3
                    ♣ 8 6 2
    ♠ Q 9 8 7 5 4          N          ♠ J 10 3
    ♡ Q                               ♡ J 10 7 5 4 3
    ◇ 10 5          W         E       ◇ K 8 7
    ♣ K J 10 7            S           ♣ 3
                    ♠ K 6
                    ♡ A K 2
                    ◇ 6 4 2
                    ♣ A Q 9 5 4
```

The rest of the hand was played in comparative silence, broken only by sporadic bursts of laughter from the Hog. Two down was the inevitable result.

As they drank champagne after the match to celebrate their victory, the Friends of Bacchus crowded round the Hog. All wanted to know what was behind his spectacular jettison of the king of clubs on the ace at trick two. Glass in hand, with the reassuring clink of ice in the bucket, the Hog was only too happy to explain.

'It was largely a question of timing,' he began. 'Had that stuffed abacus played his ace of clubs quickly, I might have been taken unawares.

'Who knows? But there he sat, thinking and thinking. What about? His opening no trump promised sixteen to eighteen points, so with that dummy, if he had the king of diamonds, I couldn't see a hope in hell of beating the contract. But if he hadn't the king of diamonds, what could be his problem? Why didn't he take a simple finesse? Clearly, he feared a bad diamond break and was looking for some other way of ensuring nine tricks. Since he hadn't held up the king of spades, I guessed that he had a doubleton and that suggested a five-card minor.

'So,' pursued H.H., 'I was fully prepared for that ace of clubs. In fact, since I think faster than he does, I knew he'd play it before he knew it himself. That's the beauty of mathematicians. Unlike human humans, they are entirely predictable. All you need do is to stand by with a banana skin. They'll slip on it every time and tell you, what's more, the exact odds against their breaking a leg.'

21. Animal Law

'That insufferable pedant!' The Hideous Hog was incensed.

'And what has the Professor done to you this time?' asked Oscar the Owl.

'Browbeating that poor Toucan, waving the law book at him,' fumed the Hog. 'Such a friendly, pleasant, clubbable member, too, and all because, to save time, he tabled his hand and claimed, without making a statement. Believe it or not, that odious Secretary Bird stopped him from drawing trumps, and not only did the Toucan go down, but he was so rattled that he lost 500 on the next hand and misdefended the one after, too. All in all, allowing for side effects, I reckon he was done out of the best part of 100 points that rubber. And he has no redress. Disgraceful!'

Oscar the Owl looked at him quizzically. 'Who was his partner?' he asked, impressed by the Hog's unaccustomed solicitude for Timothy the Toucan.

The Hog brushed that aside. 'Purely incidental. I've lost rubbers before and can take the rough with the smooth. But,' he went on raising his voice, 'I'll pay him out in his own coin. I'll show him how to apply his laws. I'll...'

Not long after this conversation, the Hog, waiting to cut in, was kibitzing a rubber in which the Emeritus Professor of Bio-Sophistry, better known as the Secretary Bird, was playing with Walter the Walrus against the Rueful Rabbit and Timothy the Toucan.

As I walked up, the Professor was dealing, cigarette in hand, flicking ash all over the table as was his custom. The Walrus protested loudly. 'A filthy habit,' he bellowed, scooping up the ash with a card, 'and if you must poison your lungs, not to mention ours, why should the cards be contaminated as well?' I took a seat behind the Rabbit and glanced at the score. Both sides were vulnerable with R.R. and T.T. 30 up in the rubber game.

```
                    ♠ 7 3
                    ♡ A 10 2
                    ◇ 10 8 7 6 4
                    ♣ 7 4 2
     ♠ 6 4                          ♠ 10 9 8 2
     ♡ K Q J 4          N           ♡ 9 7 6
     ◇ A K 5        W       E       ◇ Q 9 2
     ♣ Q J 10 8         S           ♣ 6 5 3
                    ♠ A K Q J 5
                    ♡ 8 5 3
                    ◇ J
                    ♣ A K 9
```

West	North	East	South
S.B.	T.T.	W.W.	R.R.
1♡	pass	pass	dbl
pass	2◇	pass	3♠
all pass			

The Secretary Bird led the ◇K, on which W.W. played the deuce, and continued with the ◇A.

The Rabbit ruffed and drew trumps, the Walrus following all the way. The Professor, having started with a doubleton, discarded the ♡4, then the ♣8. From dummy the Rabbit threw the ♡2 and the ♣2.

After playing quickly to the first few tricks it was the Rabbit's practice to make a plan, and he now took stock. At first sight all was well for he had four losers only, two hearts, a club and the diamond lost at trick one. And yet, a cross-check showed no more than eight winners and that struck him as odd.

'Dummy has a surplus card,' he announced after a careful recount. 'In fact,' he added, looking around the table, 'you all have too many cards.'

'If I may intrude,' ventured a junior kibitzer diffidently 'there's a blue card on top of the red pack. I didn't like to say anything before,' he went on nervously, 'as I'm a trespasser, so to speak, since I don't usually kibitz for such high stakes, but I did notice this gentleman,' he pointed to the Walrus, 'place the card there inadvertently, the three of diamonds it was, when he removed the cigarette ash which, er....'

'A revoke has been clearly established,' broke in S.B. 'Law 64 applies: when play ceases two tricks will transferred to the non-offending side and...'

'No, no,' interrupted the Walrus, 'I'm partly to blame. We both are. Let's reconstitute the second trick and say no more about it. I wouldn't like...'

With an imperious gesture the Professor stopped him. 'The law,' he proclaimed, 'knows no likes and dislikes. To condone one breach is to encourage others, and that is the road to anarchy.'

'It's most embarrassing,' protested the Walrus. 'What do you think, H.H?'

'The Professor is right,' replied the Hog. 'Your sentiments do you credit, Walter, but every player is responsible for his own cards. The revoke has certainly been established.'

I thought I could detect a malevolent gleam in the Hog's eye.

'I must insist...' began the Professor.

'You don't have to' said the Rabbit, cutting him short. 'I neither ask for favors, nor will l accept them. All I want to know whether or not this little diamond is an exposed card, and should be played at the first opportunity.'

'Yes,' said the Hog firmly.

'No,' said S.B. 'Declarer can...'

'A truce to all this wretched quibbling!' cried the Rabbit. 'Here it is. Exposed or not, I'm playing it. So there!' Whereupon he banged the ◊3 down on the table.

The Walrus won the trick with his ◊Q and after fingering a heart, returned a club. It could make no difference which card he played.

The Rabbit won, crossed to the ♡A and cashed two good diamonds. The Secretary Bird had a heart to throw on the first one, but was hopelessly squeezed by the next diamond, this being the three-card ending:

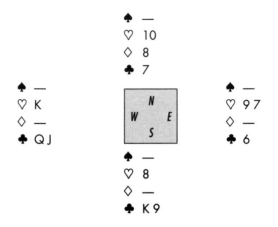

```
                    ♠ —
                    ♡ 10
                    ◇ 8
                    ♣ 7

    ♠ —                            ♠ —
    ♡ K           ┌─────────┐      ♡ 9 7
    ◇ —          N│         │      ◇ —
    ♣ Q J      W │    E    │      ♣ 6
                  │   S     │
                  └─────────┘
                    ♠ —
                    ♡ 8
                    ◇ —
                    ♣ K 9
```

The Hog was wreathed in smiles. 'Eleven tricks made and two transferred to the other side, leaving nine. Well played, R.R. And congratu-
lations to you, Professor, on your lofty principles. You realized from
the first, of course, that the contract is unmakeable and that had you
agreed to Walter's sporting offer to reconstitute the second trick they
would have gone one down. In no way could declarer avoid losing two
diamonds, two hearts and a club.

The revoke cost two tricks but brought in three — the two diamonds, which otherwise couldn't be established, and the heart or club
resulting from the squeeze engineered by you against yourself.

'Sooner than forego a penalty, you preferred to lose the rubber, and
all to stop us sliding into anarchy. Meanwhile, it's a table up, I believe.
One in.'

The wild tufts of hair over the Secretary Bird's ear bristled angrily,
but much as he hated the Hog he couldn't fault his analysis.

A STRAIGHTFORWARD HAND

The Toucan and the Walrus cut out. The Hog and the Chimp came in. This was one of the early deals:

Neither Vul.
Dealer North

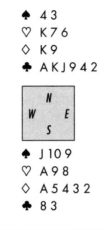

```
                    ♠  4 3
                    ♡  K 7 6
                    ◇  K 9
                    ♣  A K J 9 4 2

            N
          W   E
            S

                    ♠  J 10 9
                    ♡  A 9 8
                    ◇  A 5 4 3 2
                    ♣  8 3
```

West	North	East	South
H.H.	S.B.	R.R.	Ch.Ch.
	1♣	pass	1◇
dbl	pass	1♠	1NT
pass	3NT	all pass	

The Hog led the ♠K on which the Rabbit played the ♠8. It looked as if the hand would require a modicum of luck, a 4-4 spade break and the ♣Q on the right side. A straight-forward hand in which technique would play no part.

The ♠A, then the queen, quickly followed the king, the Rabbit echoing with the six and five.

At trick four, H.H. produced an unexpected card — the ♣Q.

Pleasantly surprised, the Chimp stretched out for the ♣A, but as he did so a question mark began to form in his mind. Why was H.H. being so helpful? To his fingers, which had already detached the ace, the brain was ending a message. Beware of Greeks bearing gifts.

'Arranging,' muttered the Chimp lamely as he replaced the ♣A.

'Arranging, fiddlesticks! You've played the card,' snorted the Walrus, who didn't like the Chimp.

Oscar the Owl hooted in disapproval.

Peregrine the Penguin raised a critical flipper.

'You played so quickly...' began the Chimp looking sheepishly at the Hog.

The Hog was unusually accommodating. 'I do tend to play too quickly at times,' he admitted, 'but I've no wish to rush you, Charlie. Take your time.'

The Chimp was deep in thought. What made the Hog play the ♣Q? Then, suddenly, the scales fell from his eyes. Of course, that was it. Realizing that the Rabbit could have no high-card entry to his two good spades, H.H. saw just one chance of putting him in — the ♣10. If the Hog had the bare queen, R.R. would have four clubs, and if so, a certain entry, for without the clubs the contract couldn't be made. It was an ingenious defense, but there was a simple counter to it — to allow the ♣Q to hold the trick.

While the Chimp pondered, the Secretary Bird, with an unfriendly gleam behind his pince-nez, generated suspicion laced with venom. Without a doubt there was dirty work afoot. But what was it? Why was the Hog being so magnanimous?

He didn't have to wait long for the explanation. Having, as he thought, divined the Hog's intentions, the Chimp played low from dummy. The Hog quickly gathered the trick, remarking pleasantly 'before he changes his mind,' and threw the ♣2 gauntly on the table. One down.

This was the deal:

```
                ♠ 4 3
                ♡ K 7 6
                ◇ K 9
                ♣ A K J 9 4 2

  ♠ A K Q 2          N          ♠ 8 7 6 5
  ♡ Q 10 5 4                    ♡ J 3 2
  ◇ Q J 10     W         E      ◇ 8 7 6
  ♣ Q 10             S          ♣ 7 6 5

                ♠ J 10 9
                ♡ A 9 8
                ◇ A 5 4 3 2
                ♣ 8 3
```

'Let this be a lesson to you, Professor,' he said sternly. 'It doesn't always pay to insist on your pound of flesh.'

22. Small Slams in the Menagerie

'That Guardian Angel is sailing pretty close to the wind,' began Oscar the Owl

'At times,' said Peregrine the Penguin, 'he's positively crooked.'

'An operator with a GA like that,' pursued O.O., 'would soon make a fortune in the City.'

'And keep out of jail, what's more,' rejoined P.P.

These remarks about the Rabbit's Guardian Angel were prompted by a deal with certain very unusual features.

It wasn't a high-powered game. The Rueful Rabbit and Charlie the Chimp were opposing Walter the Walrus and Timothy the Toucan.

Timothy the Toucan

The rubber started uneventfully. First the Toucan went down, then the Rabbit went down. Then the Walrus was set 500 in 3NT. The contract was sound enough, he explained, for with a combined count of 28½ there were 3 points to spare. Unfortunately, the defense took the first seven diamonds.

'Couldn't we have made six clubs?' ventured the Toucan. 'You could have ruffed the second diamond and...'

'A slam on twenty-eight and a half? I don't play that sort of game,' retorted the Walrus contemptuously.

On the next hand the Chimp was declarer in 4♠. As the Rabbit was tabling his hand, the steward brought the evening paper. Grabbing it, R.R. quickly dismissed the strikes and murders on the front page, and the murders and strikes on the other pages, to look at his horoscope. Would Nostradamus confirm the morning's message in *Stellar Secrets*? This had said: Virgo, 24th August-23rd September. A good day. Everyone will bend over backwards to help you. Lucky color — blue; lucky number — 12; lucky flower — orchid.

Dressed in a dark blue suit, with a small orchid in his buttonhole, the Rabbit turned to the astrological predictions, found his sign and read: 'Appearances may be deceptive, but fret not...'

He got no further. Taking the paper from him. and folding it neatly, the Chimp laid it down firmly on his side of the table. 'Twelve tricks,' he announced. 'No play needed. I just gave them a trump and claimed. An easy slam to reach too, had you made an effort. You should have done, you know. Do leave those stars alone, R.R., and come down to earth.'

'Sorry,' apologized the Rabbit. 'I didn't realize it would be over so soon, I mean that you'd make so many tricks that is...'

'Didn't we have the red pack?' asked the Toucan diffidently. No one paid any attention to him and he went on dealing with the blue pack. This was the deal which gave rise to so much discussion:

North-South Vul.
Dealer East

```
                    ♠ 6 4
                    ♡ A J 9
                    ◇ K Q 6 4
                    ♣ A 7 5
  ♠ Q J                          ♠ K 9 8 7
  ♡ 6 4              N           ♡ 7 5 3 2
  ◇ J 10 9 8     W     E         ◇ 7 5
  ♣ J 10 9 8         S           ♣ 3 2
                    ♠ A
                    ♡ K Q 10 8
                    ◇ A 3 2
                    ♣ K Q 6 4
```

West	North	East	South
W.W.	Ch.Ch.	T.T.	R.R.
		pass	1♣
pass	1◇	pass	2NT
pass	4NT	pass	6NT
all pass			

The Hideous Hog, waiting to cut in, was enjoying some private joke. He must have found it very amusing for he was laughing heartily.

The Walrus led the ◇J.

The Rabbit won in dummy, laid down the ace of clubs and counted his winners, a step he didn't usually embark upon till later in the play. But then he felt that he had been distrait on the previous deal and he was trying to make up for it.

He could see eleven tricks, twelve if either minor broke 3-3. The king and queen of clubs followed the ace. When, on the third round, East threw the ♠7 the Rabbit switched to hearts. On the third heart, the Walrus discarded the ♠J. On the fourth, panting, he shed the queen.

This puzzled the Rabbit and just to see what would happen, he cashed the ♠A. After an agonizing trance, W.W. parted with a diamond and now dummy's fourth diamond became the Rabbit's twelfth trick.

The Hog, still chuckling to himself waited till the score had been agreed.

'All over?' he asked. 'Then let me congratulate you. Not one of you noticed that you were playing with twelve cards each. I know that it makes little difference to some people, though I should have thought that Charlie might have spotted it,' he looked accusingly at the Chimp, and dropping his voice, muttered something about not looking a gift horse in the mouth.

'I only had five points' broke in the Walrus. 'Where are the missing cards? If I...'

'No, no,' the Hog quickly reassured him. 'You haven't lost a single point. It's not as bad as all that. It's only the rubber and the slam which you have lost, largely, I fear, as a result of a somewhat irregular distribution.'

The Hog removed the evening paper, revealing a trick on which Charlie had inadvertently placed it. It was the one trick won by the defense on the previous deal, a trump ducked by declarer. The four cards were the ten, five, three and two of spades.

The Rabbit looked relieved. 'I'm glad' he said 'that it isn't anything that mattered. Spades didn't come into it, of course, as I only made the ace, but it might so easily have been an important card...'

'I don't somehow think,' broke in H.H. 'that with those unimportant little spades around, you would have made your slam.'

'But that's absurd,' protested the Walrus. 'He made twelve tricks, so how can you take one away from him by giving him an extra card?'

'Would you like to try? We could have a Jeroboam on the result,' coaxed H.H. 'You'll be South and I'll be West.'

'And I play as I like? Very well, then, you are on.' The Walrus didn't know what a Jeroboam was, but he was now thoroughly aroused and he didn't like to be trifled with.

The deal was reconstituted, but with each player holding thirteen cards:

```
              ♠ 10 6 4
              ♡ A J 9
              ◇ K Q 6 4
              ♣ A 7 5
  ♠ Q J 3                      ♠ K 9 8 7 5
  ♡ 6 4          N             ♡ 7 5 3 2
  ◇ J 10 9 8  W     E          ◇ 7 5
  ♣ J 10 9 8     S             ♣ 3 2
              ♠ A 2
              ♡ K Q 10 8
              ◇ A 3 2
              ♣ K Q 6 4
```

Moving over to the Rabbit's seat, W.W. played out the cards in the same order as before. Then he tried cashing the hearts first. Then, starting all over again, he first took three rounds of diamonds.

Nothing made any difference. With an extra trick at his disposal, West was able to throw two spades on the hearts and still follow to the ace of spades, leaving his holdings in the minors intact.

'Amazing!' the Walrus exclaimed. 'South has lost a winner.'

'Not really,' corrected the Hog. 'South has lost no winners, but West has acquired a very valuable loser.'

'I wouldn't like to be credited with a slam which can only be made in, er, somewhat unusual circumstances,' declared the Rabbit, 'and I am sure that my partner feels as I do.'

The Chimp didn't seem to hear him.

'I don't want you to be embarrassed,' rejoined the Hog pleasantly, 'so I'll make the slam for you, this time with thirteen cards.'

'But you've just proved that it's impossible!' cried the Walrus indignantly.

'Shall we say a Methuselah on it?' suggested the Hog in his silkiest voice.

The Walrus bellowed with rage, but it didn't amount to acceptance of the wager.

'Please tell me how I would have played with thirteen cards?' pleaded the Rabbit.

'Certainly.' The Hog was ready to oblige. 'All you would have done,' he explained, 'would have been to restore the status quo, so to speak. At trick two, you would have led your deuce of spades, away from the ace. Opponents would have picked up the trick, of course, placing it, if you like, under Nostradamus, where we found it just now. With those four unimportant little spades out of the way, you would have played as before.'

Again they went through the motions. With his idle card removed and the count rectified, West was squeezed once more in the minors.

'Isn't that what's known as a submarine squeeze?' asked the Owl when he was discussing the hand with the Penguin.

'I'm not sure,' replied P.P. 'But submarine or no submarine, that Guardian Angel can certainly dive pretty low.'

23. Memories in the Menagerie

Over a bottle of Bollinger at the Griffins, Oscar the Owl, our Senior Kibitzer, and Peregrine the Penguin, his opposite number at the Unicorn, were reminiscing about the days of yore when they were young and strong, sowing wild oats in forever fertile soil. Amorous adventures in Capri and Cannes, drinking champagne out of ladies' slippers in the Montmartre, soon gave way to happy memories of indiscretions at the bridge table.

'Psyching was all the rage then,' the Owl was saying.

'Yes,' agreed the Penguin, 'one thought nothing of opening on a blizzard third in hand.'

'Or of making inhibitory bids on worthless doubletons,' rejoined O.O.

'It didn't pay, of course, but it was exciting,' said P.P., with a nostalgic sigh.

Glass in hand, the Hideous Hog approached their table. 'Excuse me for barging through the generation, so to speak,' began H.H., who was months younger than either of the others, 'but I couldn't help overhearing what you were saying. I quite agree. Psyching proved too expensive because, as with other pleasures, it was so difficult to practice in moderation. But though times have changed, the players haven't, and if psychic bids have been crowded out by the plethora of conventions, which make all further confusion unnecessary, psychic plays are very much in vogue. And there is, of course, the same urge to be clever for the sake of being clever, not so much to achieve anything in particular as to enjoy the stimulation.

'Now take anti-discovery plays. Very much the in-thing, you know,' pursued the Hog, scribbling on the back of the bar bill.

Neither Vul.
Dealer South

♠ Q 10 2
♡ J 3 2
◇ 8 6 4 2
♣ A 10 9

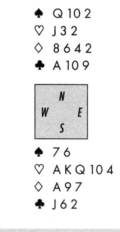

♠ 7 6
♡ A K Q 10 4
◇ A 9 7
♣ J 6 2

West	North	East	South
			1♡
pass	1NT	pass	2♡
all pass			

'West leads the king of diamonds. You win, draw trumps in three rounds, West shedding a club, and exit with a diamond to West's ten. He cashes the diamond queen, then the king of spades and continues with the jack of diamonds which you ruff. You have seven top tricks. Where will you look for the eighth?'

The Owl blinked. The Hog turned on him severely. 'I wish you wouldn't always interrupt, Oscar. It breaks my chain of thought. As I was about to say,' pursued H.H., 'you hoped that diamonds would break 3-3. They haven't, but you can still play for split honors in clubs, losing only when East has both. That's obviously the best bet, or rather it was before West played the king of spades. Can you see why?'

The Penguin opened his mouth.

'No? Then I'll tell you,' went on H.H. 'There was no need at all for West to touch spades and every need, if he had the ace-king, not to show them to me. But of course he didn't have the ace. He knew, however, that I couldn't have it either, for I had shown up already with five good hearts and the ace of diamonds. The temptation to lay down the king, as a cunning anti-discovery play, was too much for him. But in yielding to it he told me where the jack was, for holding AKx(x) any self-respecting defender would lead the x. Only from KJx(x) would the clever play of the king make sense.'

The Hog quickly filled in the diagram:

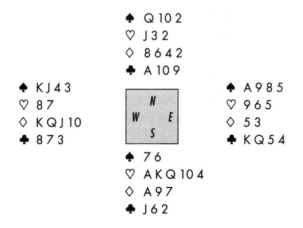

```
                    ♠ Q 10 2
                    ♡ J 3 2
                    ◇ 8 6 4 2
                    ♣ A 10 9
    ♠ K J 4 3                          ♠ A 9 8 5
    ♡ 8 7               N             ♡ 9 6 5
    ◇ K Q J 10     W        E         ◇ 5 3
    ♣ 8 7 3            S              ♣ K Q 5 4
                    ♠ 7 6
                    ♡ A K Q 10 4
                    ◇ A 9 7
                    ♣ J 6 2
```

'Left to my own devices,' said the Hog, 'I would have surely played on clubs and lost. Fortunately, I had on my left a player who was prepared to pay the price for being clever. It can be a very expensive business, you know.'

No sooner had the Owl ordered a second bottle than another diagram appeared before us:

Dealer South

                    ♠ A K J 7 3
                    ♡ 3
                    ◇ J 8 2
                    ♣ A K Q 10

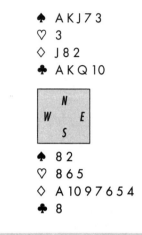

                    ♠ 8 2
                    ♡ 8 6 5
                    ◇ A 10 9 7 6 5 4
                    ♣ 8

West	North	East	South
			3◇
pass	3♠	pass	4◇
pass	5◇	all pass	

'West leads the queen of hearts. East overtakes with the king and returns the four of spades. How do you play the trumps?'

The Owl cleared his throat.

'Wrong as usual,' went on the Hog. 'Other things being equal you
finesse of course, and so long as East follows you can't go wrong. It's an
elementary safety play. But here other things aren't by any means equal
for the return of the spade suggests a singleton, and if so, you can't afford to lose a trump trick to West. Do you then lay down the ace, losing
only if East started with all three trumps, a mere eleven percent chance?
You do?' went on the Hog before anyone could reply. 'What, then, if
East is simulating a singleton to stop the impending finesse?'

'Well what if he is?' asked Oscar the Owl. 'How can you tell?'

'You can't,' replied the Hog. 'East has put you to a nasty guess and
that is all there is to it. When this hand came up I happened to be East.
Declarer looked at me suspiciously, but laid down the ace just the same.
My hand was:

♠ 9 4   ♡ A K 7 4 2   ◇ K Q 3   ♣ J 4 3

'There's nothing wrong with being clever,' concluded the Hog modestly, 'as long as one isn't too clever.'

With a hasty glance at the bottle he wrote down another deal:

North-South Vul.
Dealer South

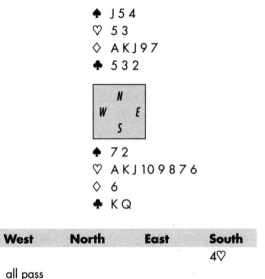

```
        ♠ J 5 4
        ♡ 5 3
        ◇ A K J 9 7
        ♣ 5 3 2

            N
         W     E
            S

        ♠ 7 2
        ♡ A K J 10 9 8 7 6
        ◇ 6
        ♣ K Q
```

West	North	East	South
			4♡

all pass

'You may think,' said the Hog, 'that this is very similar to the last deal, but there is, I assure you, a vital difference.

'I was South,' he continued. 'No one likes preempting on so strong a hand, but at unfavorable vulnerability, I knew that partner would allow for it and I didn't want the opponents to find a cheap sacrifice. The point of the hand, however, is in the play. West started with the king, then the queen of spades, East following with the three and six. Next came the jack of clubs to East's ace. At this point East led, or rather dropped, the eight of diamonds.'

'Dropped?' repeated O.O.

'Did you say 'dropped'?' echoed P.P. 'Do you mean that it fell out of his hand, so that being an exposed card it had to be played?'

'That's what it looked like, though I couldn't be sure,' replied the Hog. 'But you see the implications? East·could place every card in my hand. If I had a third spade West would have cashed his ace. The play to previous trick marked me with two clubs, the king and the queen, and I surely needed an eight-card suit for my bid, which would leave me with precisely one diamond. At this stage only a trump trick could break the contract. If West had the king or ace he would make it any-

way. So all would hinge on the queen. Normally, I would lay down
the ace-king and drop it. But what if, as on the last hand, East had the
three missing trumps? Seeing West show out the first time, I would
cross to dummy with my singleton diamond and finesse. Removing
that diamond, before I tested the trumps, would prevent the second
round finesse.

'So?' asked the Hog rhetorically.

The Owl looked inscrutable. The Penguin concurred.

'Again, as on the last hand,' pursued H.H., 'it could work both
ways. East could be pretending to have three trumps to induce a losing
finesse, or else he could be trying to protect his queen by stopping the
finesse. On the face of it, it was a guess — if East played the eight of
diamonds. If he dropped it, accidentally, the finesse would be wholly
against the odds. But there was a third possibility, that he had the
queen to three hearts and wanted, therefore, to stop the finesse without
putting me on my guard. So in playing that diamond he made it look
like an accident and...'

'A most unethical maneuver,' broke in the Owl. 'No Griffin would
sink so low. Who was East?'

'That's just it. I had never seen him before. The hand came up in
a teams event on the Continent,' explained the Hog. 'Fortunately, it
was the tenth or eleventh board, and though I knew nothing about our
opponents, I had had an opportunity earlier in the match to make a, er,
discovery play. See if you can spot it.'

```
              ♠ J 4
              ♡ A K Q
              ◇ 10 8 6
              ♣ A 10 7 6 5

                    N
                W       E
                    S

              ♠ A K Q 10 6 5
              ♡ J 5 4
              ◇ 7 3 2
              ♣ 8
```

'I was declarer in four spades. Opponents began with the three top
diamonds and switched to a club. How do you go on?'

The Penguin looked bemused.

'But there's nothing left to do,' he said at length. 'You simply claim.'

The Hog shook his head. 'Very thoughtless,' he said. 'It costs nothing to find out a little about your opponents and it can be very useful, as it proved to be on this occasion. After the ace of clubs, I laid down the ace of spades, and crossing to dummy, led the jack. East followed quickly enough, but with just that faint, all but imperceptible fumble which might have betrayed the presence of the queen. So, you see, my discovery play brought a rich reward — on that four hearts which came a few deals later. I knew that East was both clever and unscrupulous and that he had allowed that eight of diamonds to fall out of his hand deliberately, I finessed and it was as I thought:

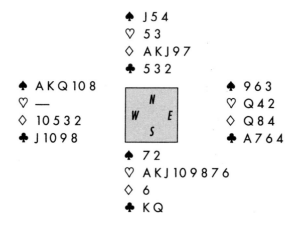

♠ J 5 4
♡ 5 3
◇ A K J 9 7
♣ 5 3 2

♠ A K Q 10 8
♡ —
◇ 10 5 3 2
♣ J 10 9 8

♠ 9 6 3
♡ Q 4 2
◇ Q 8 4
♣ A 7 6 4

♠ 7 2
♡ A K J 10 9 8 7 6
◇ 6
♣ K Q

'Was East a very young player?' asked P.P. The Hog nodded.

'Perhaps,' said the Penguin charitably, 'he was still sowing his wild oats.'

24. Bad Feelings in the Menagerie

'Now let me see...,' mused Oscar the Owl. 'Where shall I begin?'

'At the beginning,' suggested Peregrine the Penguin.

'No,' O.O. shook his head. 'It began long before that. In fact, we should go back to the day before when the Hog was playing with Colin the Corgi against Papa and the Secretary Bird.'

The Penguin had missed the meeting of our Monster Points Committee, summoned in special session to hear a charge of gross impropriety against the Hog brought jointly by Papa and the Emeritus Professor of Bio-Sophistry, known on account of his habits and appearance as the Secretary Bird. Over a bottle at the Griffins Bar the Owl was bringing the Penguin up to date.

'This was the overture, so to speak,' began Oscar, passing round the familiar diagram:

Neither Vul.
Dealer South

```
                        ♠ A J 3
                        ♡ 10 8 6 3
                        ◇ J 4 2
                        ♣ K J 10
     ♠ 10 8 5 2              ┌─────────┐
     ♡ 5 2                   │    N    │
     ◇ K 8 6             W   │         │   E
     ♣ 9 7 6 2              │    S    │
                            └─────────┘
```

West	North	East	South
			2♣
pass	2NT	pass	3♡
pass	4♡	pass	5♣
pass	5♠	pass	6♡
all pass			

'Who's who?' asked the Penguin.

'Papa and the Hog were South and West,' replied the Owl, 'but I would rather not prejudice you by telling you just yet which was which.'

'Let's say that you are West,' went on O.O. 'You lead a trump, East following, and without further ado declarer lays down, or rather bangs down, the ace of diamonds.'

The Owl paused, arching an enquiring eyebrow.

The Penguin frowned as he pondered. 'Why doesn't he draw my other trump? And what does that play mean anyway?' he soliloquized, stroking his chin. Then his brow cleared. 'Of course, I have it,' he announced. 'It's a variation on a well-known theme. In the textbooks Axx faces Jxx. Declarer eliminates the side suits and exits, making two tricks if either defender holds at that stage a doubleton honor. The correct counter is for West to unblock by jettisoning his honor, leaving East with ◇Q(K)10 to take two tricks. Declarer, for his part should play the ace as soon as possible, before defenders see what's afoot.'

The Penguin flapped his short flipper-like arms to signify that the problem had been solved. With his glossy black mohair jacket and dark orange bow tie, mounted over a snow-white shirt, Peregrine looked more than ever like a Penguin.

'So?' persisted O.O.

'So I throw the king,' replied P.P.

'It's true that I have three diamonds instead of the doubleton honor one usually finds in textbooks, but I must look ahead. Declarer may be planning a squeeze or a pseudo-squeeze or he may be trying to locate a queen, and he will be looking for an informative discard. To keep my black suits intact for as long as possible I shall have to throw a diamond anyway. Having two to spare could be distinctly helpful, so...'

'So you've fallen for it!' broke in the Owl, filling in the diagram:

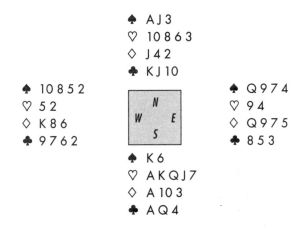

'A neat, straightforward swindle,' went on O.O. 'Looking at the two hands the contract appears to depend on the spade finesse. Finding East with a doubleton diamond honor or with both would provide additional chances. Neither, however, is particularly likely and besides, if East has the king-queen of diamonds, as well as the queen of spades, he'll be squeezed anyway. How much better to play for split honors and lay down the ace, expecting Papa, who was West as you must have guessed, to reason as you did. If he didn't fall into the trap, the spade finesse would still be there.

'That piece of hocus-pocus was a chance to nothing and it came off. Being bamboozled was bad enough,' added the Owl, 'but the manner of it, the swish of that ace of diamonds on the table, the ill-suppressed jeer, the gloating which followed, all combined to infuriate Papa and the Professor. Papa's comment was inaudible — and probably unprintable. The Professor muttered something about a tawdry three-card trick.

'That,' explained the Owl, 'was the preamble to the incident on the following day, when Papa and S.B. cut together once more against the Hog, partnered this time by Molly the Mule.'

Molly the Mule

A Two-way Finesse

I watched that rubber from the start. Everyone at the table disliked everyone else, but not in equal measure. In her disdain for men Molly was basically an egalitarian. The Emeritus Professor had been worsted by the Hog more often than by Papa and the balance of resentment showed in his manner. Papa had no reservations. He found the Hog insufferable in every position: as partner, and as opponent, and more especially as a patronizing kibitzer telling him where he went wrong. As for H.H., always broadminded, he welcomed everyone's money without prejudice, but he preferred winning from Papa since it carried the added pleasure of seeing him lose.

It was a peaceful game for the best part of ten minutes; no insults, no recriminations, nothing beyond a scathing remark or two, as often as not when the hand was over. Then came this deal:

Both Vul.
Dealer South

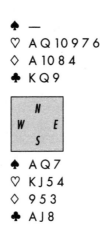

♠ —
♡ A Q 10 9 7 6
◇ A 10 8 4
♣ K Q 9

♠ A Q 7
♡ K J 5 4
◇ 9 5 3
♣ A J 8

West	North	East	South
M.M.	Papa	H.H.	S.B.
			1NT
pass	3♡	pass	3♠
pass	4◇	pass	5♣
pass	6♣	pass	6NT
all pass			

Molly led the ◊K. The Secretary Bird surveyed dummy with a certain relief. With such powerful heart support it seemed a little selfish to insist on notrump, but he wanted the lead to run up to him and he had been proved right. In hearts the slam was pretty hopeless. In notrump, on that lead, there was an excellent chance of making it. Missing the ten, Molly wouldn't have led the diamond king unless she had the jack, as well as the queen, behind it. If she also had the king of spades, she could surely be endplayed.

The Professor went up with dummy's ◊A and began to reel off the hearts, the ace, the ten then the six to the king. Always a fraction of a second ahead, H.H. followed once, then he threw the ♠2, the ♠4, and before S.B. had time to play the next card, the ♠6.

'Exposed card!' cried S.B., with a triumphant gleam in his pince-nez. 'Law Forty-nine....'

'At the Butterflies,' interjected Molly the Mule, 'we wouldn't think of enforcing such a penalty. Of course we are only a ladies' club.'

'Sorry, Molly,' apologized the Hog. 'I played too quickly. I often do, I'm afraid.'

'What do you say, Papa?' persisted the Mule, looking straight into where the Greek's eyes should be. It didn't register. Papa was busy looking for his lighter or it may have been a handkerchief.

The Secretary Bird was not to be done out of his rights. 'Law Forty-nine. The six of spades is an exposed card,' he declaimed. 'In accordance with Law Fifty it must be left face up on the table and must be played at the first legal opportunity.' He could now play either defender for the king of spades.

Despite the void in dummy, the exposed card allowed him, in effect, to finesse through East. After a moment's thought, replacing the ♡J, which he had already detached, he led the ♠Q. Molly pounced on it with the king, remarking, 'I'm glad there's some justice in the world,' and promptly cashed the ◊Q and ◊J. The full deal was this:

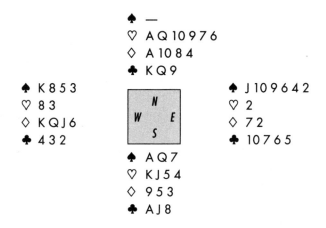

♠ —
♡ A Q 10 9 7 6
◇ A 10 8 4
♣ K Q 9

♠ K 8 5 3   ♠ J 10 9 6 4 2
♡ 8 3   ♡ 2
◇ K Q J 6   ◇ 7 2
♣ 4 3 2   ♣ 10 7 6 5

♠ A Q 7
♡ K J 5 4
◇ 9 5 3
♣ A J 8

The Secretary Bird hissed venomously. Papa exploded and forthwith lodged an official complaint.

Conducting the case for the prosecution, he told the Monster Points Committee, 'As the cards lie, the endplay against West is a certainty, but declarer doesn't know it. First, Molly must have the king of spades. Next she mustn't have four clubs. Otherwise, in the three-card ending, she can bare the spade king, retaining a diamond honour and the thirteenth club. Declarer would have to guess.

'Of course, H.H. could place every card. If the Professor had the king of spades, he had twelve top tricks. If he hadn't, he needed the queen to make up his fifteen points for a minimum strong notrump. Unable to finesse, he couldn't go wrong. So by deliberately exposing the six of spades, H.H. presented declarer with a losing option. To all intents and purposes, he could now finesse. He was given the choice, and as we all know, the Professor has a tendency to insist a shade too firmly at times on the strict letter of the law. Cynically exploiting this weakness,' went on the Greek, 'he set a trap, a cheap, transparent maneuver which a more perspicacious declarer...' The rest of the sentence was drowned as the angry, sibilant noises behind him rose to a crescendo of hissing.

Dismissing the charges against him with the polished contempt of the experienced defendant, the Hog took up Papa's phrase. 'A cheap, transparent maneuver, was it? Why, then didn't Papa support Molly's protest? Why did he look the other way? I will tell you, gentlemen. He wanted to have it both ways, to take the money if I had the king and to bring this charge against me if I hadn't.'

'I have always tried,' concluded the Hog with a lofty look, 'to set an example by being a good winner. It's up to Papa to set an example, too. He should learn how to be a good loser. Having played against me all these years, he should have had plenty of practice.'

25. Brilliant Dummy Plays

Walter the Walrus is a greatly underrated player. Of that he has never been in any doubt. It's all very well to talk sagely of trump coups and intra-finesses, but when it comes down to playing straight down the middle, counting the points and tricks, leading the fourth-highest or returning partner's suit, the Walrus considers that he can hold his own in any company. Neither is he overawed by players who talk better and faster than he does, and yet, despite all their pretensions, open on tram tickets, raise partner's suit without four-card support and discard thoughtlessly, then claim to have been squeezed. He had seen such things happen too often to be easily impressed by so called experts.

And so it was in his usual mood of quiet confidence that, when the Hog and the Chimp cut out, the Walrus joined the Rabbit and the Secretary Bird, Papa being the other newcomer to the table.

Cutting for partners was an anxious moment, for the odds were 3-1 against him. Papa was, of course, by far the best player of the three, but insisting, come what may, on being the center of attention, he made partner feel purely incidental, and the Walrus didn't like being incidental. The Rabbit was scatterbrained, dithered, and, instead of arranging his tricks neatly in front of him, shuffled them up into an untidy heap. As for the Emeritus Professor of Bio-Sophistry, commonly known as the Secretary Bird, he was as disagreeable to his partners as to his opponents. Most people play bridge for pleasure. The Professor played it for the displeasure he could cause others.

The Walrus sighed as he cut the Rabbit.

'A modest tenner on the rubber?' suggested the Hog to the Chimp. 'I'll back Walter and R.R.'

'Done!' said the Chimp with alacrity.

A junior kibitzer looked up in surprise. In the absence of the Toucan, the Rabbit and the Walrus were indisputably the worst two players in the club, if not in London. Why, then, should the Hideous Hog, who had a reputation for betting strictly with the odds, put his money on them? A more experienced kibitzer could have told him. One has to pay for one's pleasures, and how could the Hog insult Papa more effectively than by betting against him. R.R. and W.W.? A tenner? Cheap at the price.

Before long this deal came up:

Neither Vul.
Dealer South

```
                    ♠ Q
                    ♡ 10 4 2
                    ◊ K 9 4
                    ♣ A 10 8 5 3 2

    ♠ J 10 9 8          N            ♠ K 7 6 3 2
    ♡ 9 7 6                          ♡ 8 5 3
    ◊ Q J 8 7 6     W       E        ◊ A 3
    ♣ 4                 S            ♣ K 9 6

                    ♠ A 5 4
                    ♡ A K Q J
                    ◊ 10 5 2
                    ♣ Q J 7
```

West	North	East	South
S.B.	R.R.	Papa	W.W.
			1♡
pass	2♣	pass	3NT
pass	4♡	all pass	

'One heart' said the Walrus.

'Had you switched to a spade, you could have beaten that last contract,' the Chimp was saying to the Rabbit.

'Your bid!' roared the Walrus.

The Rabbit apologized and bid 2♣. A pass, 3NT from the Walrus and a pass from the Secretary Bird followed in quick succession.

'I couldn't, er, four hearts,' said the Rabbit. 'I couldn't have switched...'

The Secretary Bird hissed venomously. The Walrus glared at him belligerently. Papa tapped irritably on the table.

'Sorry, sorry,' apologized the Rabbit once again, and as the professor led the ♠J, he spread his hand with a guilty look, the club suit on the right.

'You really must think what you are doing,' spluttered the Walrus indignantly. 'It's unfair to your partner, all this jabber-jabber. Most distracting.'

Walter pulled dummy's ♠Q into the center of the table, and the king was quickly tossed on top of it. With one stopper only in spades, reflected the Walrus, everything would hinge on the club finesse, unless of course Papa had three spades only.

The hold-up at trick one was automatic. To Walter's surprise, the Greek gave his next play several seconds thought, but eventually decided to press on with spades. The Walrus ducked again, throwing a small heart from dummy. A long pause ensued.

Finally, the Walrus turned to the Professor, and was surprised to meet an equally expectant stare. 'You're on the table,' explained the Rabbit, helpfully.

'No, the eight of spades took that last trick,' Walter corrected him.

'No, no, you ruffed it in dummy,' pointed out R.R. to the accompaniment of a sibilant jeer from S.B.

'Ruffed? In 3NT?' protested the Walrus. The majority view being that the contract was four hearts, the Walrus exploded. 'Why can't you put the trumps on the right and why do you support my suit without four trumps? I might have four small to the king or to the jack for that matter. Why…'

The Walrus was fuming, but he nevertheless drew trumps and quickly lined up ten tricks — losing only a spade, a club, and the ◊A.

'All's well that ends well,' he told the Rabbit reprovingly, 'but had you not confused me I would have won the first trick, ruffed a spade, drawn trumps and…'

'And gone down like a man,' broke in H.H., finishing the sentence for him. 'No, no, Walter, you played brilliantly, if without malice aforethought. In no other way could the contract be made once they had led a spade. If you win the first trick and finesse in clubs, Papa gives his partner a club ruff, and then a diamond through the king sinks you. You can ruff one spade, but that will only yield nine tricks, and you can't ruff two because there's no way back to your hand to draw trumps without losing a club, and club ruff and two diamonds. In fact, on that line you might easily go two down. You did well, Walter.

I congratulate you, though in all fairness, R.R. deserves some of the credit, for the play no less than the bidding.'

The Chimp was about to speak. 'Will you kindly play somewhere else, while you are kibitzing?' said Papa to him tersely. 'Neither will the game be any less enjoyable if you take H.H. with you.'

The Secretary Bird dealt:

North-South Vul.
Dealer West

```
              ♠ K
              ♡ 6 2
              ◇ A 10 6 5 4
              ♣ A J 6 5 4
                   N
               W       E
                   S
              ♠ A Q J 10
              ♡ A K Q J 10 9
              ◇ Q 8
              ♣ 7
```

West	North	East	South
S.B.	R.R.	Papa	W.W.
pass	1◇	pass	2♡
pass	3♣	pass	3♠
pass	4♡	pass	4NT
pass	5♡	pass	6♡
pass	7♡	all pass	

The opening lead was a heart. Tabling his hand with tremulous fingers, the Rabbit apologized in advance. 'I know,' he began, 'that I should have three or even four points more, but that singleton king in your second suit must be worth at least two tricks, so if you can make twelve without it...'

An angry growl from the Walrus brought him to a halt.

For once the kibitzers, ignoring Papa, were crowding round him. He, not the Greek, was the center of attention and he intended to make the most of it. If he went down the blame would fall fairly and squarely on that crazy Rabbit. If he brought home the grand slam, and there was a chance, he would get the recognition that had so long been denied him.

There were twelve ready-made tricks, but if S.B. held both the $\Diamond$K and also the king-queen of clubs, he would be squeezed in the four-card ending. When the last major-suit winner touched the table, S.B. would have to come down to three cards, while dummy, poised over him, would have four — $\Diamond$A10 $\clubsuit$AJ. Whichever suit S.B. unguarded, dummy would discard from the other.

The Walrus cleared trumps in three rounds. 'Club away,' he instructed the Rabbit. Four spades followed. 'Clubs away,' went on W.W. Then, 'Diamond away,' and again, 'Diamond away'. The Rabbit complied quickly, but the Walrus was in no hurry and with slow, measured movements he reeled off the spades, then his fourth and fifth hearts. 'Diamond away,' he directed each time, his senses aroused by the authoritative tones of his voice.

As the $\Diamond$10 was whipped away, leaving the ace bare, a sudden shudder shook his frame. Beads of perspiration broke out on his forehead as he realized with a shock that he had spoken once too often. All prospects of a squeeze had gone and with them all hope of the personal triumph that would follow.

With a menacing look, he turned on the Rabbit. 'How could you throw that diamond? Whose side are you on?'

'But you told me to do it!' pleaded the Rabbit.

'Are you a robot? Have you no sense at all?' cried the Walrus. 'A slip of the tongue, a word out of place and you pounce on it to throw any chance we might have of making the contract. How could I have intended...'

'Of course not,' broke in Papa, 'and since it was purely unintentional we shouldn't take advantage of it. Take it back, Walter.'

There was a dangerous gleam behind the Professor's pince-nez. The wiry tufts of hair behind his ears bristled angrily. 'Pray be so good,' he hissed, 'as to refrain from flaunting your generosity at your partner's expense. There are laws and rules at bridge, as in the world at large, which must be observed by all if we are not to lapse into anarchy.'

'Well spoken,' chuckled the Hog with a malevolent look at Papa. This was the deal in full:

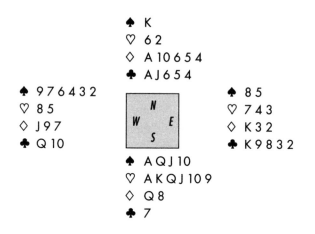

```
              ♠ K
              ♡ 6 2
              ◇ A 10 6 5 4
              ♣ A J 6 5 4
♠ 9 7 6 4 3 2                    ♠ 8 5
♡ 8 5              N             ♡ 7 4 3
◇ J 9 7       W         E        ◇ K 3 2
♣ Q 10            S             ♣ K 9 8 3 2
              ♠ A Q J 10
              ♡ A K Q J 10 9
              ◇ Q 8
              ♣ 7
```

Papa's last five cards were:

◇ K 3   ♣ K 9 8

Which should he throw?

If he let go a club, the ace, followed by a club ruff, would set up dummy's jack, and the ◇A would still be there as an entry. The ◇3 was an unassuming, inconspicuous card, so Papa shed it hopefully.

Counting, however, was the best part of W.W.'s game, and he had counted the diamonds carefully. With a whoop of triumph he laid down the ace, bringing down the lone king. The ♣A and a club ruff to hand with his last trump allowed the ◇Q to bring in the thirteenth trick.

'A trump squeeze by North against South and East. A rare coup indeed!' chortled the Hog.

'Why didn't you keep a diamond guard?' hissed the Secretary Bird. 'I carefully discarded my three diamonds to give you the count.'

Papa was spluttering with rage. 'You gave *him* the count, then you subjected *me* to a trump squeeze!' he cried.

The Walrus was shaking his head. They all make mistakes, he was saying to himself. More than ever he was convinced that he was a greatly underrated player.

26. The Greedy Double

It isn't customary to bid 7NT missing two aces. Still more unusual is it for such contracts to be redoubled. That, however, is what happened during a recent rubber at the Griffins. At the request of Papa the Greek, who claimed to be the victim, an extraordinary meeting of our Monster Points Committee was summoned to consider a situation for which there was no known precedent.

As so often happens, the scene for the deal in question had been set by the one that preceded it. It was an ordinary unfriendly game with the Hog kibitzing at the usual stakes against Papa in harness with Walter the Walrus against Charlie the Chimp and the Rueful Rabbit. Each side in turn made game, then this deal came up:

Both Vul.
Dealer East

```
                    ♠ 1098765
                    ♡ K
                    ◇ 52
                    ♣ J1098
    ♠ AQ
    ♡ AQJ109           N
    ◇ KQJ10        W       E
    ♣ KQ               S
```

West	North	East	South
Papa	Ch.Ch.	W.W.	R.R.
		pass	pass
2♣	pass	2♡	pass
4NT	pass	5◇	pass
6♡	all pass		

The Rabbit led the ◇A, followed by the ◇8. The Chimp's first card was the ◇2, then, on Papa's ◇K he discarded the ♠5.

'No diamonds, partner?' dutifully asked the Rabbit.

'No,' began the Chimp, then hastily correcting himself, he apologized and produced the ◇5.

Walrus crossed to his hand by overtaking the ♠Q with the king and continued with a heart to which the Rabbit followed with the five, Walter the Walrus paused and pondered. Clearly he had six hearts and was wondering whether to finesse or play for the drop. 'It's fifty-two to forty-eight,' he muttered, 'but which is which? For the life of me I can't remember.' Finally he finessed.

'Blast!' he exclaimed as the Chimp pounced with the king on dummy's queen. 'I should have gone up with the ace. The odds....'

'The odds have nothing to do with it,' broke in Papa angrily. 'Since Charlie couldn't ruff the second diamond — that is, while he was under the misapprehension that he'd started with a singleton — he obviously couldn't have a trump, so the finesse was mandatory.'

With a contemptuous smile Papa turned to the Chimp. 'Have you been reading any good books lately?' he asked with a sardonically-raised eyebrow. 'I seem to remember seeing this pretty play somewhere, but for the moment the title escapes me. Maybe you can refresh my memory.'

The Chimp grimaced, but his reply was inaudible. The Hog's attention was riveted on something in the *Financial Times*.

Noblesse Oblige

Blushing with embarrassment, the Rueful Rabbit drained his cherry brandy and ordered another. Unwittingly he had been a party to a piece of sharp practice. It made him squirm. Beads of perspiration rolled down his forehead as he dealt the next, fateful hand:

Both Vul.
Dealer South

```
              ♠ J 9 8 7 5
              ♡ K 9 3
              ◇ A 4
              ♣ A 8 2
  ♠ A 6 2          N
  ♡ A Q 10 7 4 2
  ◇ —        W        E
  ♣ Q J 5 4        S
```

West	North	East	South
Papa	Ch.Ch.	W.W.	R.R.
			1◇
1♡	2♠	pass	3♣
pass	3◇	pass	?

At this point, the Rabbit, still occupied with his galling experience on the last deal, asked for a review of the bidding.

'You opened one diamond,' began Papa. 'I called one heart and Charlie....'

'No, surely you called two hearts,' interposed the Chimp. Everyone assured him that he was mistaken.

'Oh sorry. Of course, I wouldn't have, well, er...' The Chimp didn't finish the sentence.

'This creates a very awkward situation,' said Papa. 'Information has been disclosed which wouldn't have normally come to light till the auction was over. We had better have a ruling.'

Halfway through a bottle of Bollinger, Oscar the Owl was summoned from the bar. Munching furiously his favourite chocolate and almond biscuits, the Rabbit awaited impatiently his pronouncement.

Having deliberated, the Owl spoke with aplomb. 'There is no law to cover this specific situation,' he said gravely, 'so we turn to the proprieties and here the right course to pursue is clear. Since it would be improper for R.R. to benefit from information conveyed in an irregular manner, he should bid exactly as he would have done had the unintentional jump to two spades not been, as it were, alerted.'

Breathing a sigh of relief, R.R. promptly bid 4NT. With the signals set at 'Danger' the Chimp applied the brakes as hard as he could with 5♣, a thoughtless act which took no account of the Rabbit's lofty principles. Rejecting the unlikely picture of an aceless hand strong enough to jump to 2♠, he proceeded on the honorable assumption that the Chimp was showing all four aces. With his eyes open and his head high, R.R. proudly bid 7NT.

'Did you have to do that?' protested the Chimp vehemently as in a soft, caressing tone Papa applied the inevitable double.

'Yes, I did,' retorted the Rabbit with spirit. 'Redouble!' And with that, his pent-up feelings found a sudden, happy release. All sense of guilt left him, for he had well and truly expiated the sins of his partner.

This was the full dramatic auction:

```
              ♠ J 9 8 7 5
              ♥ K 9 3
              ◇ A 4
              ♣ A 8 2
♠ A 6 2                        N
♥ A Q 10 7 4 2           W          E
◇ —                            S
♣ Q J 5 4
```

West	North	East	South
Papa	Ch.Ch.	W.W.	R.R.
			1◇
1♥	2♣	pass	3♣
pass	3◇	pass	4NT
pass	5♣	pass	7NT
dbl	pass	pass	redbl
all pass			

A dazzling disaster was in sight, but what lead would be most likely to lend luster? Papa considered his options and finally settled on the ♡2 to create the false picture of a balanced distribution, concealing the void in diamonds. The Rabbit played low from dummy, winning W.W.'s eight with the jack. The ♠K and then the ♠Q followed. Papa held off, while the Walrus, showing little interest in the hand, followed with the three and four. At the fourth trick the Rabbit switched to the ♣3.

Should Papa split his honors? As he explained later, that might cost a trick but could never gain one. The Rabbit would go up with the ace and clear the spades, forcing Papa to set up dummy's ♡K, or to lead into the ♣K10 in the closed hand. Conversely, if the Walrus had the ♣10, or the nine for that matter, going up with an honor would serve no purpose. So the Greek played low. The Rabbit inserted dummy's eight and was much surprised to see it hold.

After wandering towards the spades, then back to the clubs, his hand eventually came to rest on the ♢A. Four more diamonds came in quick succession.

As diamond followed diamond, Papa felt the noose tightening. This was his unenviable position when the last one appeared on the table:

```
              ♠  J
              ♡  K 9
              ♢  —
              ♣  A 2
   ♠  A        ┌─────────┐
   ♡  A        │    N    │
   ♢  —        │  W   E  │
   ♣  Q J 5    │    S    │
              └─────────┘
```

He could tell that the Rabbit had three clubs left, but what was his other card, a heart or a spade? As he meditated, the Rabbit, who had been playing at top speed, discarded dummy's ♠J. Thereupon Papa shed the ace. Parting with the ♡A or with a club would assuredly cost a trick, but the Walrus might, should in fact, have the ♠10. If so, the discard of dummy's jack, before Papa had played to the trick, made little sense, but R.R's line of play wasn't always impeccable and it was, after all a chance to nothing.

Before he gathered the trick, the Rabbit gazed intently at the ♠A. Then he played the ten and Papa was well and truly squeezed.

This was the deal:

```
              ♠ J 9 8 7 5
              ♡ K 9 3
              ♢ A 4
              ♣ A 8 2
♠ A 6 2                          ♠ 4 3
♡ A Q 10 7 4 2      N            ♡ 8 6 5
♢ —            W         E       ♢ 10 8 7 6 5 3
♣ Q J 5 4          S            ♣ 7 6
              ♠ K Q 10
              ♡ J
              ♢ K Q J 9 2
              ♣ K 10 9 3
```

'Had you split your club honors, sir,' ventured a junior kibitzer, recently promoted from watching backgammon, 'you could have broken the contract.'

'Result merchant!' jeered the Hog.

'Why did you play the three of spades before the four?' cried Papa. 'If you had three spades, as you should have done...'

'What?' broke in the Walrus indignantly. 'I hadn't a point to my name and it's all my fault, is it? How many more aces do you need to defeat 7NT on your own?'

The Chimp was busy adding up.

Papa asked the Monster Points Committee to annul the hand. The grand slam would never have been bid had the Chimp not disclosed improperly that he had misheard a bid and it was against the spirit of the laws that a player should profit from an irregularity. The redouble was a gesture, rather than a bid, provoked by a deplorable incident on the previous deal. It would be an affront to justice if the Chimp were to reap a rich reward for his unseemly conduct.

Appearing for the defense, the Hog began by rejecting the allegations against the Chimp. There being no conclusive evidence against him, he should be found not guilty and warned not to do it again. As for the grand slam, Papa's greed had proved, as so often before, to be his undoing. Not content to cash his aces and take the 1000 points which the Rabbit's reckless gallantry had put within his reach, he wanted not one pound of flesh, but two. A less rapacious defender would have started with the ♡A. Seeing the fall of the jack he would have continued with the suit, scoring six tricks in all, a penalty of 3400. Even at the end Papa could have stopped the slam by discarding a club on the last diamond. But no, like the monkey with his paw in the pouch, he wouldn't let go.

'My heart goes out to Walter,' concluded H.H., 'the innocent victim of his partner's shameful cupidity. I have no doubt, of course, that Themistocles will be glad to compensate him by paying the losses he had inflicted on him. I make the difference between the foreseeable penalty and the actual score, allowing for the rubber points, come to 6330 — or have I left something out?'

27. The Rabbit in Love

The Rabbit's heart missed a beat as he cut Dolly the Dove against the Emeritus Professor of Bio-Sophistry, commonly known as the Secretary Bird, and Molly the Mule. Somehow Dolly made him feel that she liked playing with him. It was a weird sensation. She was never rude or scathing to him. Not once had she lost her temper. Unaccustomed to such favors, R.R. determined to live up to them.

A second cherry brandy, another of his favorite chocolate and almond biscuits, and he was ready for the fray. Most of his lapses, he felt, were due to lack of concentration. He had read many learned works and he had on his shelves both the British and American editions of the *Official Encyclopedia of Bridge.* On the theoretical side there weren't too many chinks in his armor. It was just that he occasionally slipped up in practice.

'Blind man's bluff,' said the Hog to the Chimp as they strolled into the room. 'They probably think they're playing bridge.'

'Like a bet?' suggested the Chimp. 'It will give us an interest. Usual club stakes. I'll take the Mule and the Secretary Bird unless you'd rather...'

'No, no,' the Hog shook his head. 'I couldn't bear to be on the same side as that pedant. Give me the Rabbit. The Devil, they say, looks after his own.'

Before long, this deal came up:

Neither Vul.
Dealer North

<pre>
              ♠ 4 3
              ♡ A 10 6 5
              ◊ A K 3 2
              ♣ J 6 3
                  ┌───────┐
                  │   N   │
                  │ W   E │
                  │   S   │
                  └───────┘
              ♠ A K Q J 10
              ♡ K 8
              ◊ J 10 4
              ♣ 8 7 4
</pre>

West	North	East	South
S.B.	R.R.	M.M.	D.D.
	1◊	pass	1♠
pass	1NT	pass	4♠
all pass			

The Secretary Bird led the ♣K, the ♣A and a third club to Molly's queen. Back came a trump.

'Seems to depend on the diamond finesse,' whispered the Chimp.

'There's the added chance that a ruff could bring down the queen-jack of hearts,' pointed out H.H.

Dolly didn't bother about such things. She played out her trumps quickly and confidently. Reeling off winners was a pleasant pastime; while it lasted. Each defender followed three times. The Rabbit, watching every eyelash, anticipating every move, matched speed with speed, detaching one card after another.

On the third round of trumps, Dolly called for a heart from dummy, on the next one for a diamond. Then came the last trump and the Rabbit threw another diamond, baring the ace-king, when a startled

'Oh!' from Dolly stopped him in his tracks. She'd already led the ◊J to the next trick before the previous one had been turned.

The Rabbit hastily withdrew the diamond.

'That card has been played,' said S.B. firmly.

'I hadn't called for it,' protested the Dove.

'You had played to the next trick,' persisted S.B.

'I wouldn't like to take advantage,' began Molly with a wan smile.

'Thank you, Molly,' said Dolly. 'Of course, I didn't intend.....'

'You had played to the next trick' hissed the Secretary Bird. 'The rules are made to be followed — by everyone,' he added, looking sternly at R.R.

'Bad luck, Dolly,' said the Chimp, backing him up.

'But I hadn't played to the trick,' protested Molly.

A rasping noise from the back S.B.'s throat reminded her that she was supposed to be on his side.

The Rabbit looked appealingly at the Hog. He was always meticulous in serving the proprieties, but the anguished thought that he had let down the Dove brought beads of perspiration to his forehead.

'Molly is quite right and her sentiments do her credit,' said H.H., who had been watching her intently. 'She is too generous to take advantage of a trifling, meaningless slip. But,' went on the Hog, 'by the same token, Dolly cannot accept such favors. Technically, she was at fault, so I fear that the diamond has been played.'

'On the other hand,' countered the Chimp, changing sides quickly, 'Molly can't be compelled to enforce a penalty. Besides, she herself hasn't yet played to that trick.' He wasn't at all sure why the Hog seemed to be arguing against his own interests, but he trusted his judgment. Whatever was good for the Hog the opposite must be good for Charlie the Chimp.

'True,' agreed the Hog with a mischievous glance at the Mule. 'Molly can withdraw any card she would have played and substitute any other. She is free to do absolutely anything.' The Hog found it hard to suppress a chuckle — or maybe he didn't try.

Molly was in dire trouble. Having started with:

♠972 ♡QJ42 ◊Q98 ♣Q92

she could afford to part with a heart on the fourth trump. But now this was the six-card ending:

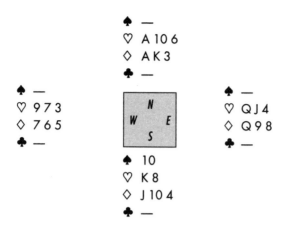

$\spadesuit$ —
$\heartsuit$ A 10 6
$\diamondsuit$ A K 3
$\clubsuit$ —

$\spadesuit$ —
$\heartsuit$ 9 7 3
$\diamondsuit$ 7 6 5
$\clubsuit$ —

$\spadesuit$ —
$\heartsuit$ Q J 4
$\diamondsuit$ Q 9 8
$\clubsuit$ —

$\spadesuit$ 10
$\heartsuit$ K 8
$\diamondsuit$ J 10 4
$\clubsuit$ —

What could she throw on the next one after the Rabbit's unauthorized discard of a diamond?

All set to beat the contract had the diamond finesse been taken as declarer intended, Molly was caught in a squeeze from which there was no escape. The $\diamondsuit$10 brought Dolly her tenth trick.

'A criss-cross squeeze by dummy,' observed Oscar the Owl, 'a very unusual maneuver.'

THE RABBIT MAKES A VOW

The Rabbit motioned to the steward for another cherry brandy. Heaving a sigh of relief, he made a vow: never, never to tempt Providence again. From now on he would concentrate for all he was worth.

Molly dealt. 'One spade,' said the Rabbit concentrating on his vow.

'Bid out of turn,' snapped the Secretary Bird. 'Do you know the penalty or shall I...'

'No, no,' implored the Rabbit, turning from crimson to scarlet. 'I know everything. I mean Dolly can't say anything, the bidding reverts and I...'

'Pass,' said Molly firmly.

Dolly shook her head wistfully.

'Pass,' said the Secretary Bird with an angry glint in his pince-nez. He hadn't forgotten the last deal.

The Rabbit, last to speak, was looking at:

$\spadesuit$ K J 9 7 5 $\heartsuit$ Q J $\diamondsuit$ 4 $\clubsuit$ K 9 6 5 4

Since no one had found a bid, Dolly was marked with a fair hand and could, in fact, have a powerhouse. Fortified by the third cherry brandy he took the plunge: 'Four spades.'

For the first time since the rubber started the Secretary Bird's thin bloodless lips curved upwards in a smile as, with a triumphant look at his enemies seated around him, he doubled. This was the deal:

North-South Vul.
Dealer East

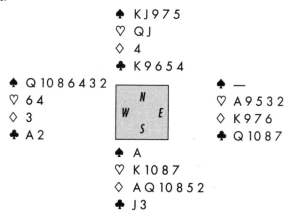

```
                    ♠ K J 9 7 5
                    ♡ Q J
                    ◊ 4
                    ♣ K 9 6 5 4
♠ Q 10 8 6 4 3 2                        ♠ —
♡ 6 4                N                  ♡ A 9 5 3 2
◊ 3             W         E             ◊ K 9 7 6
♣ A 2                S                  ♣ Q 10 8 7
                    ♠ A
                    ♡ K 10 8 7
                    ◊ A Q 10 8 5 2
                    ♣ J 3
```

Molly led a club to S.B.'s ace. A second club came back.

The Rabbit went up with the king and continued with the ♡J, ducked by Molly. The diamond finesse followed, then the ◊A, on which he threw a heart, and a heart ruff in the closed hand. Next a club was ruffed with dummy's ace, and underruffed perforce by S.B. Then another heart, ruffed and overruffed. Having made seven tricks, R.R. remained with ♠KJ9, ♣96. Exiting each time with a club, he couldn't be denied three more tricks for his contract.

'Why didn't you go up with the ace of hearts?' hissed S.B. 'How many tricks did you expect to take with it?'

'Is that why you didn't play a trump at trick two?' retorted Molly. 'You wanted to do him out of the ace, I suppose?'

Dolly was beaming at the Rabbit. His heart missed another beat.

28. Concentrating on the Improbable

It had been a pleasant dinner. The Hog, the Owl, the Penguin and Colin the Corgi, the facetious young man from Oxbridge, did full justice to a quail stuffed with *foie gras aux truffes de Perigord*, matched by a La Tache '70, so reminiscent of the great vintage of '61. As the port circulated around him the Hog was in a benign, discursive mood.

'Have you considered,' he philosophized, 'how many words, how many figures, how many decimal points are lavished on tables of odds and probabilities? All those dreary statistics indicating the likelihood of this or that hand pattern, of finding doubleton queens and singleton kings. What a waste of space.'

'But surely,' objected Peregrine the Penguin, 'you can't deny that it is helpful to know these things?'

'I do deny it,' rejoined H.H. with spirit. 'We all know that a finesse is more likely than a 3-3 split. Such things we learn at kindergarten. But if we clutter up our minds with trivia we have less energy, less time left to draw inferences, to make deductions, to plan ahead, in short, to play bridge. All those unlikely probabilities,' added the Hog decisively. 'Concentrate on the improbable and let the probable take care of itself.'

'A splendid epigram,' interjected the ever sarcastic Corgi, 'but what, if anything, does it mean? How do you concentrate on the improbable?'

'Give me a scrap of paper and I'll show you,' replied H.H.

The Corgi produced a notebook and tearing out a gilt-edged page presented it to the Hog. 'There,' said H.H., quickly sketching in the North-South hands over the familiar diagram:

Both Vul.
Dealer North

```
            ♠ 10
            ♡ Q J 9
            ◇ Q 10 5 3
            ♣ A Q 10 4 3
            ┌───────┐
            │   N   │
            │ W   E │
            │   S   │
            └───────┘
            ♠ A
            ♡ A 10 8 6 4
            ◇ J 9 4
            ♣ K J 5 2
```

West	North	East	South
Papa	R.R.	Karapet	H.H.
	1♣	pass	1♡
pass	2♡	pass	3♣
pass	3♡	pass	3♠
pass	4♣	pass	4♡
all pass			

'This hand came up at Thursday's duplicate at the Unicorn,' he explained. 'Everyone was in four hearts. I happened to have Papa on my left. He started with a low diamond to Karapet's king. A diamond went back to Papa's ace and a third diamond was ruffed by Karapet, who returned a club. Over to you.' The Hog looked enquiringly round the table.

'A fiendish defense,' said Oscar the Owl.

'I don't suppose anyone else found it,' echoed Peregrine the Penguin.

'Fiendish, perhaps,' said C.C., 'but not so very improbable. The bidding pointed to a gap in diamonds and leading low from the ace was likely to induce the wrong guess if the king were in dummy and declarer had the jack, while if partner had the king it might not matter either way.'

'Perhaps so,' agreed the Hog. 'But now, since Papa did find what Oscar has described as a fiendish defense, how do you proceed?'

The Owl hooted softly.

'That's not an answer,' objected H.H.

'I win on the table and run the queen of hearts hoping for the best,' said P.P. 'What else am I supposed to do?'

The Corgi looked noncommittally supercilious.

'How about hoping to drop the bare trump king?' suggested the Hog.

'If the hearts break 3-2' countered O.O., the king is more likely to be guarded twice than once. So the odds are six to four on the finesse. If the suit is divided 4-1 the odds...'

'No, no, Oscar,' protested the Hog. 'Stop thinking of your silly tables. No matter how the trumps split West must have the king. The finesse is doomed.'

'East is just as likely as West to have the ♡K. It's about fifty-fifty,' declared the Penguin defiantly.

'What you are saying, little though you realize it,' retorted the Hog, 'is that because of your blind faith in probabilities you insist on taking a finesse, propelling yourself, like a lemming, to destruction, unable or unwilling to stop in your tracks.'

'But surely...,' broke in the Owl.

'Not at all.' The Hog raised an imperious finger. 'If the finesse succeeds, every South in the room will make eleven tricks. You alone will be kept to ten. At best you'll share a bottom with some other luckless declarer who will come up against the same inspired defense. Your only hope is to find West with the king of hearts.'

'Then you'll make nine tricks while everyone else will make ten,' insisted the Penguin, unwilling to surrender.

'Only if I finesse,' replied H.H., 'but I don't. I lay down the ace of hearts hoping to find the bare king. The odds aren't so bad anyway, but I'd play the same way if they were ten to one against me, for I have nothing to lose and a lot to gain — and for once,' added the Hog, 'justice was done and could be seen to be done.'

This was the full deal:

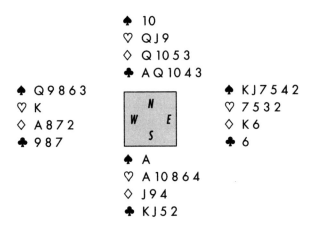

	♠ 10	
	♡ Q J 9	
	◇ Q 10 5 3	
	♣ A Q 10 4 3	
♠ Q 9 8 6 3		♠ K J 7 5 4 2
♡ K		♡ 7 5 3 2
◇ A 8 7 2		◇ K 6
♣ 9 8 7		♣ 6
	♠ A	
	♡ A 10 8 6 4	
	◇ J 9 4	
	♣ K J 5 2	

'As you can see' concluded the Hog, 'I backed the improbable because it was chance to nothing. You were so preoccupied with the probable that you overlooked it.'

HOPING FOR THE WORST

Buoyed up by the appearance of a second decanter the Hog accepted another leaf from C.C.'s notebook and was soon in full spate again.

East-West Vul.
Dealer East
North-South 70 on

♠ Q 2
♡ 3 2
◇ J 10 6 5 2
♣ K Q 3 2

♠ K 4
♡ A 8 5
◇ A K Q
♣ 9 8 7 6 5

West	North	East	South
W.W.	T.T.	Ch.Ch.	H.H.
		1♡	2♣
pass	pass	2♠	pass
3♠	4♣	all pass	

'Of course,' said H.H., 'that ridiculous Toucan should have bid three clubs the first time to make life harder for the Chimp. The point of the hand, however, is in the play. The Walrus leads the jack of hearts. I win. What next?'

Glass in hand the Hog sat back.

'If the Chimp has ♣AJ(10)x over dummy there's nothing we can do about it, so we hope for a 2-2 trump break. It may sound too simple but I lead a club.'

'Impossible,' chipped in the Corgi. 'H.H. would never have put the question if that was to be the answer.'

'At trick two I led the king of spades,' said the Hog, ignoring him.

'Why?' enquired the Penguin suspiciously.

'Just routine,' explained H.H. 'It couldn't lose and there was always the chance that the Chimp would do something useful, like leading a trump. However, he didn't, so it doesn't matter. He went up with the ace of spades, cashed the king of hearts dropping Walter's ten and exited with a spade to dummy's queen.'

'So we are back to square one,' said the Owl. 'We might just as well have played a trump from hand at trick two. We do so now hoping, as before, for a 2-2 break.'

'You play an honor from dummy and hope for a 2-2 split? Is that right?' The Hog looked around for signs of dissent. There were none.

'Just as I thought,' sighed the Hog. 'Far from trying to avoid defeat, which is staring you in the face, you are positively wishing it on yourselves. Don't you see what will happen if your hopes are realized?'

'But what else are we supposed to do?' asked the Penguin who was getting more than a little confused.

'You must take your one and only chance and lead a low club hoping, not for a lethal 2-2 split, but for a bare ace.'

'And is it likely?' asked the Penguin.

'Not so very unlikely,' rejoined the Hog 'but that, again, is irrelevant, because against your probable 2-2 split you have no chance at all. The Chimp will go up with the ace of trumps and lead a third heart for Walter to ruff, forcing out dummy's queen or king of clubs. Because of your unhealthy preoccupation with those probabilities, you find yourselves hoping for an uppercut to knock you out. As on that other hand I showed you, you couldn't see the facts through the figures.'

These were the four hands:

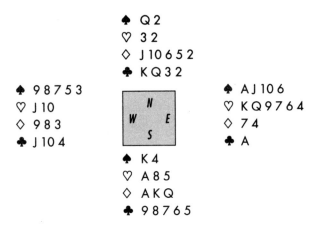

```
              ♠ Q 2
              ♡ 3 2
              ◇ J 10 6 5 2
              ♣ K Q 3 2
♠ 9 8 7 5 3        N        ♠ A J 10 6
♡ J 10          W     E     ♡ K Q 9 7 6 4
◇ 9 8 3            S        ◇ 7 4
♣ J 10 4                    ♣ A
              ♠ K 4
              ♡ A 8 5
              ◇ A K Q
              ♣ 9 8 7 6 5
```

The Hog frowned. 'Who invented these mini decanters, I should like to know? I'll swear this one never held a full bottle.'

'Another case of the improbable,' suggested Colin the Corgi.

29. The Cards Take Charge

'Do you think that the cards have a soul?' asked the Rabbit, thoughtfully sipping his Chateau d'Yquem.

Oscar the Owl's round amber eyes opened wide. He was too preoccupied with his *crêpes Suzette* to do more. Not so Peregrine the Penguin. A rationalist, who had inherited a keen sense of logic from his French grandmother, he deprecated all fantasies. 'Cards are inanimate. Therefore, if there is such a thing as the soul, which is debatable, the cards cannot have one,' he pronounced authoritatively. Most of the Penguin's announcements were authoritative.

'Well, then,' persisted the Rabbit, 'is there some sort of force following a course of its own, if you see what I mean?'

'I certainly don't,' replied the Penguin. 'You have probably imbibed too freely of that excellent Ladoucette with the *sole Veronique*, but there's no sort of occult force. The cards dance to your tune. You don't dance to theirs,' he added sententiously.

'It could be the Guardian Angel,' ventured the Owl, who had dispatched the last of the *crêpes*.

'I'm afraid I am no good at explaining things,' said the R.R. turning towards me in exasperation. 'You saw those two hands we discussed at dinner last night, when the cards kept doing their own thing, just as if I wasn't there. Uncanny wasn't it? Tell them about it.'

Ignoring a derisory squeak from the back of the Penguin's throat, I tried to put the Rabbit's thoughts into words.

'There are times,' I explained, 'when R.R. sees the cards as a *boutique fantasque* coming to life, every character following, or so it seems, the movements he directs, and yet unwittingly, he is doing someone else's bidding. That is what R.R. means by a "force following its own course".'

'If it's not the Ladoucette, it's the artichoke he had for starters that's gone to his head,' was the Penguin's scathing comment.

'Tell them about those hands,' pleaded R.R. We had gone through them at length together, so I remembered them well. The first one came up during an ordinary unfriendly rubber in which the Rabbit and his friend Timothy the Toucan were playing against Molly the Mule and Charlie the Chimp.

Both Vul.
Dealer West

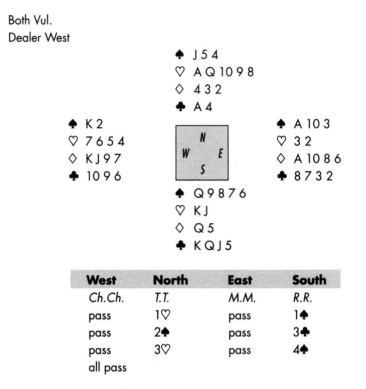

```
                    ♠ J 5 4
                    ♡ A Q 10 9 8
                    ◇ 4 3 2
                    ♣ A 4
    ♠ K 2                              ♠ A 10 3
    ♡ 7 6 5 4          N              ♡ 3 2
    ◇ K J 9 7      W       E          ◇ A 10 8 6
    ♣ 10 9 6          S              ♣ 8 7 3 2
                    ♠ Q 9 8 7 6
                    ♡ K J
                    ◇ Q 5
                    ♣ K Q J 5
```

West	North	East	South
Ch.Ch.	T.T.	M.M.	R.R.
pass	1♡	pass	1♠
pass	2♠	pass	3♣
pass	3♡	pass	4♠
all pass			

The Chimp led the ♣10.

The Rabbit could see at a glance that he had four losers, two diamonds and two trumps, three unless he could successfully circumnavigate the ♣10. Fortunately the lead gave him a chance to get rid of a diamond loser on one of dummy's hearts. So, rising with the ♣A, he started with three rounds of hearts. Before he could discard a diamond, however, Molly ruffed the third round with the ♠3 and R.R. had to overruff.

Next the Rabbit turned to clubs, throwing a diamond from dummy on the third round. On the fourth club the Chimp found himself in a cleft stick. Unless he ruffed, another diamond would be discarded from dummy and R.R. would be able to ruff a diamond. And if the Chimp ruffed with the ♠K it would be a case of killing a loser with a winner. So, perforce the Chimp ruffed with the ♠2. Overruffing in dummy the

Rabbit tried another heart, hoping that the Mule had started with a doubleton king or ace. Molly, however, ruffed with the ♠10 and once again the Rabbit had to overruff, bringing about this five-card ending:

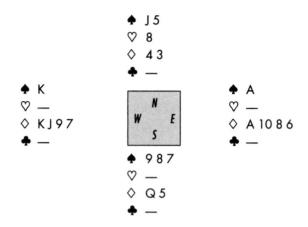

With nothing left to ruff anywhere it didn't matter much what he did next, so the Rabbit led a spade and, much to his surprise, the king and ace came toppling over each other.

Molly was quick off the mark. 'I must say, partner, you found a most unimaginative lead. They bid every suit but diamonds, so a diamond lead surely stood out a mile.'

'I, too, know what to lead when the hand is over,' countered the Chimp. 'I couldn't guess...'

'Of course not,' broke in Molly the Mule, 'that would have required a speck of commonsense, not one of the innumerable gifts for which the dominant sex is renowned.'

There was a lot more of it, but the Rabbit wasn't listening. He had more than enough to worry about his own mistakes without bothering about other people's. Besides, Molly's partners always made mistakes. He sometimes wondered why she ever played with them.

What the Rabbit couldn't understand about the hand was that once again the cards had 'taken charge' as he put it. 'Of course I expected to lose two tricks to the ace and king of trumps,' he explained, 'but from trick one I did all I could to get rid of a losing diamond. But see what happened. I lost two diamonds, but the ace and king of trumps somehow telescoped into one. It doesn't happen to other people,' he concluded ruefully.

'I still think it's the Guardian Angel,' said the Owl. 'I wouldn't put it past him. He ought to be in the City. He'd soon have the pants off those whiz-kids.'

'Blind man's buff,' scoffed the Penguin.

'Tell them about the other hand,' insisted R.R. 'How often can lightning strike in the same place?'

The hand in question came up the very next day at the Unicorn's weekly duplicate. I noted it down at the time.

The Rabbit, once more in harness with the Toucan, was moving for the last round, when he overheard the Hog, passing by him, tell the Corgi, 'We are running neck and neck, but Themistocles meets the Rabbit in the last set, which gives him the edge, of course, so we'll have to pull something out of the bag.'

As Papa and Karapet took their seats, R.R. was on his mettle. He would be the one to pull something out of the bag.

The first of the two boards they had to play was flat. The Greek made ten tricks in 3NT, a dead average. This was the last board:

North-South Vul.
Dealer South

```
                  ♠ K 10 3
                  ♡ 7 6 4 2
                  ◇ A Q
                  ♣ A Q 5 3
  ♠ J 8 2                        ♠ Q 4
  ♡ A K Q 3          N           ♡ 10 9 8 5
  ◇ 9 7 5        W       E       ◇ J 10 3 2
  ♣ J 8 6            S           ♣ 10 9 7
                  ♠ A 9 7 6 5
                  ♡ J
                  ◇ K 8 6 4
                  ♣ K 4 2
```

West	North	East	South
Karapet	T.T.	Papa	R.R.
			1♠
pass	2♣	pass	2◇
pass	3♠	pass	4NT
pass	5♡	pass	6♠
all pass			

Timothy's jump to 3♠ proclaimed three-card support and at least a game-going hand. Now the Rabbit, the Hog's words still ringing in his ears, went in search of higher things rather than sign off tamely in game. When Timothy showed only two aces the Rabbit reluctantly settled for the small slam.

Karapet led the ♡K, then the ♡A. The Rabbit ruffed, and resisting the temptation to take a couple of rounds of trumps before looking further afield, counted his losers and winners. There was one loser too many and two winners too few. Assuming a normal break, a trump loser was inevitable, but an extra winner could, perhaps, be conjured up.

The Rabbit had read many articles on dummy reversals and his studies now proved their worth. Going over first to the ◊Q, then to the ◊A, he ruffed two more hearts in his hand. Next he 'finessed' the ♣Q, cashed the ♣A and came back to hand with ♣K, hoping that Papa, duly deceived, wouldn't ruff if he had no more clubs. All followed, however, and the ◊K brought him his ninth trick, dummy shedding the last club. With the ♠A and ♠K still intact his objective had been achieved. He wouldn't go more than one down.

This was the three-card ending:

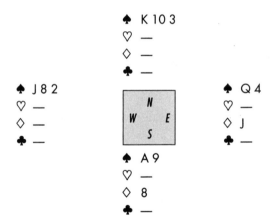

```
                      ♠ K 10 3
                      ♡ —
                      ◊ —
                      ♣ —
   ♠ J 8 2          ┌─────────┐          ♠ Q 4
   ♡ —              │    N    │          ♡ —
   ◊ —              │ W     E │          ◊ J
   ♣ —              │    S    │          ♣ —
                    └─────────┘
                      ♠ A 9
                      ♡ —
                      ◊ 8
                      ♣ —
```

Without malice aforethought R.R. played the ◊8. Sighing, the Armenian inserted the ♠8. The ♠10 won the trick.

The Rabbit was both gratified and perplexed. 'I wonder what happened to that trump loser?' he mused aloud. 'I suppose if you score enough winners first it doesn't matter what happens to the losers. And yet, you know,' he added ruefully, 'it's not what I had set out to do, was it?'

The Rabbit had planned to go one down on a dummy reversal, instead of which he had made his contract by a Devil's Coup. Once more, the cards had 'taken charge'.

When I finished my story, I turned to the Penguin. 'Do you see now,' I asked him, 'what R.R. means when he sees a mysterious force propelling his cards?'

'Well, there may be something to be said for the Devil,' concluded P.P. grudgingly, 'but as for that Angel, it's all stuff and nonsense.'

30. The Papadopoulos School of Thought

As always when the Fates and Furies brought the Hog and Papa face to face, kibitzers from the four corners of the card room gathered round them. Griffins at the bar hastily emptied their glasses to watch the duel. Before long this deal came up:

Both Vul.
Dealer North

```
        ♠ Q 10 6 4
        ♡ A 10 7 5
        ◇ K 10 9
        ♣ 7 2
```

```
        ♠ A K 7 2
        ♡ —
        ◇ A J 3
        ♣ A K Q 10 8 6
```

West	North	East	South
Papa	R.R.	Karapet	H.H.
	pass	pass	1♣
pass	1♡	pass	2♠
pass	3♠	pass	4◇
pass	4♡	dbl	5♣
pass	5◇	pass	6♣
dbl	6♠	all pass	

Papa led the ♡2, low from dummy, the ♡J from Karapet.

The Hog ruffed and laid down the ♠A on which the Armenian threw the ♡3. So, thought the Hog, that's why Papa had doubled 6♣. Since Karapet couldn't have a spade he would have made a Lightner double and raised the alarm. By forestalling him Papa would protect him, and if, as in the event, the Rabbit panicked and bid 6♠, that was something which, sitting with five trumps, Papa could contemplate with equanimity. It was out of notrump that the Greek wanted to steer the enemy and in that he had certainly succeeded.

After the ♠A the Hog continued with the ♠K, then the ♠7, finessing the ♠10. Next he cashed the ♠Q, carefully watching Karapet's discards. They were the ◊4, ◊5 and ◊6. Evidently he could afford no more hearts. The Hog paused. His beady eyes narrowed. Then leering triumphantly at Papa, he led the ♣7, and when the Armenian played low, he ran it!

This was the deal in full:

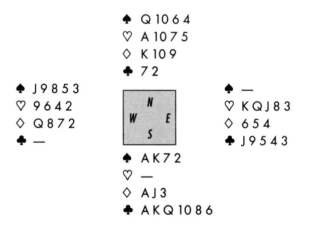

                    ♠ Q 10 6 4
                    ♡ A 10 7 5
                    ◊ K 10 9
                    ♣ 7 2

    ♠ J 9 8 5 3   ♠ —
    ♡ 9 6 4 2   ♡ K Q J 8 3
    ◊ Q 8 7 2   N   ◊ 6 5 4
    ♣ —   W   E   ♣ J 9 5 4 3
                       S

                    ♠ A K 7 2
                    ♡ —
                    ◊ A J 3
                    ♣ A K Q 10 8 6

Papa could score his fifth trump when he liked, but there was no other trick for the defense.

Later in the bar we quizzed H.H. about his spectacular play in clubs. What made him do it? The Hog was only too anxious to explain.

'I counted Karapet's hand,' he told us. 'Clearly he had five hearts, not six, or he could have afforded to discard another. But that left four to Papa and he had led the two of hearts. How very unlike him, I thought, to lead a true card. And that gave me the vital clue. That two of hearts was a compulsory true card. He had no choice. Karapet's double of four hearts might well have shown the ace, and if so, Papa wanted a club back, and he couldn't signal for it without the indignity of leading a true card. Now everything fell into place. And to think,' chortled the Hog, 'that I might have been left to play in six clubs. Knowing nothing of the distribution I might well have gone down.'

THE RABBIT APOLOGIZES

I was reminded of this deal by one which came up a few days later in the weekly duplicate at the Unicorn.

Delayed by a *bécasse au fumet* which took longer than usual to prepare, I didn't get to the cardroom till the tournament was well under way. As I approached the door I could hear the Mule upbraiding the Walrus. 'Had you not been so busy miscounting my points you might have realized that my two of diamonds wasn't a come-on card...'

I reached Molly's table just as the players were taking the cards out of their slots:

East-West Vul.
Dealer West

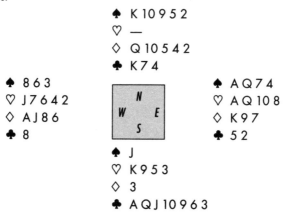

```
                ♠ K 10 9 5 2
                ♡ —
                ♢ Q 10 5 4 2
                ♣ K 7 4
♠ 8 6 3                          ♠ A Q 7 4
♡ J 7 6 4 2          N           ♡ A Q 10 8
♢ A J 8 6       W        E       ♢ K 9 7
♣ 8                  S           ♣ 5 2
                ♠ J
                ♡ K 9 5 3
                ♢ 3
                ♣ A Q J 10 9 6 3
```

The Secretary Bird, South, was playing with a guest from Burundi, whose name I didn't quite catch, except that it began with Totsi.

West	North	East	South
W.W.	Totsi	M.M.	S.B.
pass	pass	1NT	3♣
3♡	5♣	all pass	

The Walrus led the ♢A, then switched to his singleton trump. Winning in hand the Secretary Bird played the ♠J. Molly came in with the ♠Q and returned her second trump. With two trump entries in dummy S.B. had no difficulty in catching the ♠A, getting back to dummy with a heart ruff and parking his other heart losers on the spades.

'Must be a dead average,' said Molly. 'They can hardly stay out of five clubs and as the cards are the hand plays itself.'

'With only nineteen points between them,' growled the Walrus, 'they...'

The rest of the sentence was drowned by a popping champagne cork. It came from across the room where the Hog and the Corgi were opposing Lord Mortsbury, President of International Morticians Inc., and his export manager, Jeremy Joybell. The champagne, Louis Roederer's Crystal, I noticed later, was on an expense account, of course. As the board was being moved from the Mule's table to theirs, I followed the sound of the cork.

The contract was the same as at the other table and so was the play to the first two tricks. Unlike Molly, however, the Hog allowed the ♠J, at trick three, to win. With only two entries in dummy, Mortsbury couldn't set up the spades and get back to enjoy them. He could ruff two hearts, of course, but that still left two heart losers. One down.

'An average,' said, or rather announced, the Hog.

Mortsbury shook his head. 'Not everyone will duck that ♠J,' he said. 'We were unlucky to have come up against one of the few players who would.'

The Hog brushed this aside. 'Elementary. Kindergarten. Why, even Papa couldn't fail to make the right play,' he added, raising his voice so that the Greek, who was within earshot, could hear him.

'I'm not so sure,' said Joybell. 'Let's see what the traveling scoresheet says.'

The Hog dismissed that as irrelevant. He had pronounced one down to be the average. If the traveling scoresheet didn't bear it out, so much the worse for the sheet.

'Please move for the last round,' called the Tournament Director. I followed the board to the Rabbit's table. Sitting East in harness with the Toucan, he was up against Charlie the Chimp and his Australian cousin, Vera the Vixen.

The contract was again 5♣, and again the defense started with the ◊A followed by a trump. Unlike the other declarers, however, the Chimp won this in dummy and with studied nonchalance led the ♠2. The Rabbit played low automatically and the Chimp, smirking gleefully won the trick with his singleton jack. The Vixen smiled approvingly.

The crafty Chimp had induced the guileless Rabbit to put up the same defense as the Hog had done, and the contract could no longer be made.

'One down,' said the Chimp. 'With four top losers that can't be bad, especially as they can make four hearts. Should be well above average.'

While the Rabbit was apologizing for his thoughtless play, Vera was looking at the traveling scoresheet. 'A tie for bottom,' she read out with pursed lips. 'Only one other declarer went down and two North-Souths scored 200 and 500 respectively, defending against four hearts doubled.'

The Hog was much amused when I told him about the Chimp's discomfiture.

'Just like that Rabbit,' he chuckled. 'Does the right thing inadvertently, would like nothing better than to take it back, and shares a top with me as the result. Mind you,' went on H.H., 'had the opening lead been a heart, Charlie's play would have been correct. Now, unless the queen of spades goes up, declarer can ruff three hearts in dummy, losing only one heart and one diamond. And if the spade queen is played, dummy's two entries suffice to bring in the spades.

'That Chimp,' concluded the Hog, 'belongs to the Papadopolous school of thought, but whereas Themistocles is subtle and imaginative, the Chimp is merely crude and cunning. I sometimes wonder, you know, why I bother to take his money.'

Karapet, the Unlucky Armenian

31. A One-Sided Match

HH DANS LES VIGNES DU SEIGNEUR RETOUR RETARDE REGRETS — DUPONT

The cable bearing this cryptic message was handed to Oscar the Owl, our Senior Kibitzer, barely an hour before the annual match between the Bacchanalians and the Dionysians was due to begin. In plain English it meant that the Hog was suffering from an acute hangover and would not be back in time for the match. The signatory was the organizer of the Wine Festival at Beaune.

The Hog had been invited to serve on the Jury and there is no doubt that he had discharged his duties conscientiously — too conscientiously, by all accounts. We learned the details later. The immediate problem was to find a replacement. Gavin the Goose, who was having a late lunch, was the only candidate on the premises and he was far from enamored of competitive bridge. It was so unlike baccarat.

Oscar, who was in charge of the tournament, tried to flatter him.

'I wouldn't ask anyone else to take the Hog's place' he began, making a virtue of necessity.

The Goose was hesitant, but as they chatted news came through that Papa had just arrived, and on hearing that H.H. couldn't make it, was laying seven to four against the Bacchanalians.

G.G. began to take an interest. 'If I string him along, he's so conceited that I might get two to one, maybe even nine to four.'

O.O. heaved a sigh of relief. The crisis was over, but there could be little doubt that what had promised to be a close match would be a very one-sided affair. Without the Hog, the Bacchanalians would be heavily outgunned.

In the first half the Rueful Rabbit and Gavin the Goose faced Molly the Mule and Timothy the Toucan. One or two lucky misunderstandings on mostly flat hands kept the lead of the Dionysians down to under 200. Then, towards the end of the session, this deal came up:

Neither Vul.
Dealer South

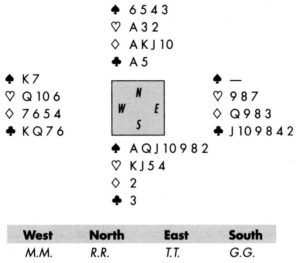

```
              ♠ 6 5 4 3
              ♡ A 3 2
              ◇ A K J 10
              ♣ A 5
♠ K 7                              ♠ —
♡ Q 10 6           N              ♡ 9 8 7
◇ 7 6 5 4      W       E          ◇ Q 9 8 3
♣ K Q 7 6          S              ♣ J 10 9 8 4 2
              ♠ A Q J 10 9 8 2
              ♡ K J 5 4
              ◇ 2
              ♣ 3
```

West	North	East	South
M.M.	R.R.	T.T.	G.G.
			1♠
pass	2◇	pass	4♠
pass	6♠	all pass	

Molly led the ♣K. The Goose rose with dummy's ace, lost a trick to the king of trumps, and after trying unsuccessfully to bring down the ◇Q, lost the finesse in hearts. One down.

Molly wasn't slow to point out that had he taken a ruffing finesse in diamonds he would have made the contract.

'How was I to know...?' began G.G.

'You can't always know,' retorted the Mule with a superior smile. 'It's a question of intuition, something men don't understand. Take that hand I had at the Butterflies last Sunday, when...'

I missed the story as I carried the board to the other room, where there had been a crisis.

A few minutes earlier a garbled telephone message from a Ukrainian house-porter came through to say that a pipe had burst in the flat above Karapet's and that the water was pouring through the ceiling. Which ceiling? It wasn't clear. It could be over the room housing the Armenian's priceless *Sèvres* china. Karapet couldn't wait to get back and for the last set of boards his place was taken by the Secretary Bird. Papa made no attempt to hide his disappointment. As I placed the board on the table, he was muttering something unpleasant in Greek.

The contract was the same as in the other room, and like Molly, Charlie the Chimp, sitting West, led the ♣K.

The Greek glanced at his wristwatch. 'We are running late,' he said, 'so I won't waste time over this kindergarten hand. Unless Walter has a singleton diamond, which is most unlikely, a simple elimination ensures the contract.' As he spoke Papa faced his cards.

'No one has a singleton diamond,' said Walter the Walrus, 'but how do you propose to avoid the loss of a spade and a heart if Charlie has the king of spades and queen of hearts, well-guarded, of course?' The Walrus wasn't going to be talked out of anything.

'How tiresome of you Walter,' replied Papa. 'I was only trying to save time, but I'll go through the motions if you insist. I go up with the ace of clubs, ruff a club with the eight and cash the ace and king of diamonds. Now I lead a trump. If you follow I finesse. Charlie can make his bare king, but must now lead into my heart tenace, present me with a ruff and discard or set up a diamond for me in dummy. If you show out in spades I play the ace and throw Charlie in on the next round, which will come to the same thing.'

'And how do you propose to reach dummy's diamond if Charlie sets it up for you?' persisted the Walrus. His suspicions had not been allayed.

'With the deuce of spades, of course,' replied Papa irritably. 'I did tell you that I would ruff dummy's five of clubs at trick two with the eight. Evidently you missed the implications.'

The Walrus gave Papa the sort of look a dishonest servant would expect if he hadn't been caught out in something. A surly growl conceded the contract.

'Can't think why they took so long over it in the other room,' said Papa. 'It wasn't as if there was some way of going down.'

JUPITER IN THE ASCENDANT

'Let's change places,' suggested the Rabbit to the Goose, as they were about to enter the second half. 'It may bring us luck.' His horoscope for the day had said distinctly 'An unscheduled change will lead to unexpected results'.

On a succession of small, flat hands the Dionysians more than held their own and when the last board was placed on the table their lead had risen to 1920.

Both Vul.
Dealer North

```
              ♠ A 8 7
              ♡ A Q 3 2
              ◇ K 8 6
              ♣ A K J
♠ 9                           ♠ K J 10 6 5 4 3
♡ J 10          N             ♡ 9 8 7 6
◇ 10 5 4 3    W   E           ◇ 2
♣ Q 9 7 6 4 2     S           ♣ 10
              ♠ Q 2
              ♡ K 5 4
              ◇ A Q J 9 7
              ♣ 8 5 3
```

West	North	East	South
Ch.Ch.	T.T.	W.W.	M.M.
	2NT	pass	3◇
pass	3♡	pass	4♡
pass	4♠	dbl	pass
pass	5♣	pass	6◇
all pass			

The slam was an eminently sound one.

East's helpful double of 4♠, pinpointing the king, made it cast iron. Even without the tell-tale double, either a 3-3 heart break or the club finesse would ensure twelve tricks. The Chimp led the ♠9, making assurance doubly sure. Molly played low from dummy, losing the trick to the king. The Walrus returned another spade and just as the Mule was about to spread her hand the Chimp ruffed.

'What infernal bad luck,' exclaimed Molly. 'A 7-1 break is less than a three percent chance, and of course there was no other way to play it.'

'Of course not,' agreed the Toucan, anxious as ever to please.

'Sympathy!' Molly oozed contempt from every pore.

The Toucan felt very, very guilty.

Admittedly that spade break was a straightforward case of bad luck, but one, I couldn't help reflecting, which the Dionysians could well afford, for even if they bid and made the slam in the other room, the swing wouldn't suffice to close the gap.

I took the board across. Like the Toucan, the Goose opened 2NT and the first three rounds of bidding were the same. When the double of 4♠ came round to him, however, G.G. did not bid 5♠ as T.T. had done. He pondered deeply. Then having made up his mind, he closed his cards, put them down and announced, '*Banco!* Six diamonds. What the hell, nothing venture nothing win!'

There was a dangerous gleam in S.B.'s pince-nez. 'I protest' he cried. 'This is highly improper. By gesture and word of mouth you are telling your partner that you have made the final bid. I have no alternative but to invoke Law Sixteen.'

Papa, who had been growing increasingly restless, tried to stop him, but there was no holding back the Emeritus Professor of Bio-Sophistry. Drawing the book of Laws from an inside pocket he deftly turned the pages and read out, 'Law Sixteen. *Unauthorized Information*: If a player conveys information to his partner by means of a remark... special emphasis, tone, gesture, movement, mannerism that suggests a call, lead or play...' S.B. paused before resuming in solemn tones of a judge passing sentence, 'either member of the non-offending side may prohibit any call or play so suggested.'

Again Papa tried to intervene, but to no effect.

The Secretary Bird turned to the Rabbit. 'Your partner has indicated unmistakably that he has made the final bid and desires you to pass. I prohibit you to pass.'

'What then, must I bid?' asked R.R., his head in a whirl.

'Anything you like,' rejoined S.B., 'so long as you do not pass.'

The Goose looked shocked. It was as if with 8 or 9, he had been ordered to draw a card at baccarat.

'Why,' said Papa *sotto voce*, 'couldn't a pipe have burst over his ceiling?'

The Rabbit considered his options. With nothing in clubs, 6NT was out of the question. Hearts? The Goose didn't seem keen on them. Maybe it wasn't even a suit. You never knew these days. That only left diamonds. So, in a tremulous voice, with downcast eyelashes, he murmured, 'Seven diamonds.'

As in the other room the lead was the ♠9. In a grand slam there could be no question of ducking, so the Rabbit went up with the ace and began to count. He could see eleven top tricks, so it only needed the club finesse and a 3-3 heart break to bring the total to thirteen. He had been in many a worse contract. The Rabbit's ears twitched excitedly. With Jupiter in the ascendant and Venus rising he might wipe that sneer off S.B.'s face.

After four rounds of trumps he took the unavoidable club finesse, and as he fully expected, it came off. The ♣A and ♣K followed, S.B. shedding spades. Back in hand with the ♡K he cashed the last trump. This was the four-card ending:

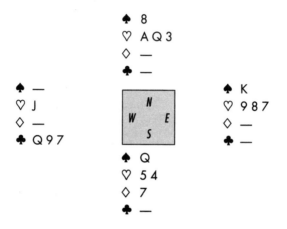

The ♠8 was thrown from dummy and S.B. hissed, but then he always did. The Rabbit wasn't watching the discards. He knew in his bones that the hearts would break and so they did, of course.

The Bacchanalians had won by 220.

The Goose was looking even more pleased with himself than usual. Virtually single-handed he had won the match and he had squeezed 9-4 out of Papa.

Before long menacing sounds could be heard from the passage. The Greek and the Mule were berating the Secretary Bird. A most enjoyable cacophony, thought Gavin the Goose.

32. The Impressionist School of Bridge

The Hog maintains that he can diagnose most hands as soon as dummy goes down. Even Papa, he says, knows what's happening after three or four tricks have been played. Lesser mortals, of course, have to wait till the post mortem. The Rabbit is altogether different. With a style all his own, he rarely knows more about a hand after it has been played than he did before. As an ardent disciple of the Impressionist school of bridge. he believes in bold splashes of color. Not for him the tedious minutiae of counting every card and every situation in slavish obedience to the mystic sign of 13.

Two deals which occurred on successive days, and were not wholly unrelated to each other, illustrate his approach to the game.

The first came up at the Unicorn's weekly duplicate. I first saw it played from a seat behind the Hog:

Neither Vul.
Dealer West

```
                    ♠ A 3 2
                    ♡ A K 4 3
                    ◇ 6 4 3
                    ♣ 6 4 2
    ♠ K Q 10 9 6 5                      ♠ J 8 7
    ♡ J 6 5            N                ♡ 10 9 8 7
    ◇ Q J          W       E           ◇ 10 9 8
    ♣ K Q             S                ♣ J 10 9
                    ♠ 4
                    ♡ Q 2
                    ◇ A K 7 5 2
                    ♣ A 8 7 5 3
```

West	North	East	South
S.B.	C.C.	Ch.Ch.	H.H.
1♠	pass	pass	dbl
pass	2♠	pass	3◇
pass	3♡	pass	4♣
pass	4◇	pass	5◇
all pass			

The Secretary Bird led the ♠K to dummy's ace.

Summing up the position at a glance, H.H. ruffed a spade, cashed the ♣A, then the ◇AK and proceeded with three rounds of hearts. When all followed, he exited with a club. With only spades left, S.B. hissing as was his wont, had no option but to concede a ruff and discard. The Hog ruffed in hand, discarding dummy's last club, and ruffed a club for his eleventh trick.

As the cards lay, cashing the ♣A at trick three was an unnecessary precaution, but the Hog didn't want to alert S.B., who, with ♣Kx, would doubtless have unblocked had the elimination of the side suits warned him of the impending endplay.

On the opening the traveling scoresheet we found that several other Souths played in 5◇, but only one, the Rueful Rabbit, made it. I wondered what happened and during the interval I sought out the Rabbit, congratulated him on his play and asked for the details.

The Rabbit, who had played the board against Papa and Karapet, was nonplussed by my enquiry. 'But there were eleven top tricks,' he replied, 'so what's all the fuss about?'

'Which eleven tricks?' I asked.

The Rabbit reeled them off quickly. 'The ace of spades and two ruffs, the ace, king, queen of hearts, that's six, four trumps, assuming a 3-2 break, that's ten and the ace of clubs. What more do you want?'

'But you can't count two spade ruffs *and* four trumps,' I protested. 'You are counting the same trumps twice.'

'Yes, yes,' R.R. wasn't going to be bogged down in trivia, 'but for all that, you know, Papa didn't find the best defense. When he came in with his king of clubs he played a spade, which, of course, gave me a ruff and discard. I suppose he was playing a forcing game, but it only goes to show that even the best players make mistakes. Had Timothy or I done anything like that we should never have heard the end of it.'

A Spade to Spare

Back to rubber bridge at the Griffins the next day, R.R. cut Walter the Walrus against Papa and Karapet. Soon this deal came up:

Neither Vul.
Dealer East

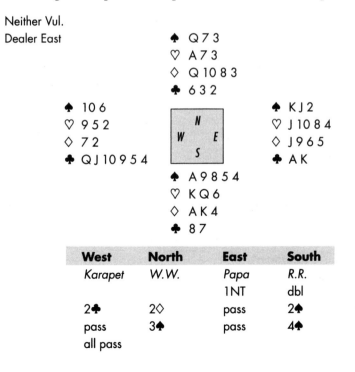

	♠ Q 7 3	
	♡ A 7 3	
	◇ Q 10 8 3	
	♣ 6 3 2	

♠ 10 6		♠ K J 2
♡ 9 5 2		♡ J 10 8 4
◇ 7 2		◇ J 9 6 5
♣ Q J 10 9 5 4		♣ A K

	♠ A 9 8 5 4	
	♡ K Q 6	
	◇ A K 4	
	♣ 8 7	

West	North	East	South
Karapet	W.W.	Papa	R.R.
		1NT	dbl
2♣	2◇	pass	2♠
pass	3♠	pass	4♠
all pass			

Papa had a regulation weak notrump, but he has been known to take liberties against lesser players and this may have prompted R.R. to bid the fourth spade. Anyone could go down with dignity, but it was humiliating to be bounced out of a game by a specious notrump.

'If you have your bid you should have no trouble,' said the Walrus, putting down his hand.

Karapet led the ♣Q. Papa overtook with the ace, cashed the king and switched to a diamond.

I watched the hand closely and could find no fault with the Rabbit's play from here, but the rationale behind it mystified me.

'When there's no other way,' he whispered to me when he saw dummy, 'play for a mistake.' What did he mean? I wasn't aware of any mistakes. In the bar, later, over the pre-prandial Bollinger, I asked him to explain.

'Well,' he began, 'I had already lost two tricks and I could hardly avoid losing two more in trumps, not by legitimate means, anyway.

'I suppose that Papa could have had a doubleton king of spades, but he clearly had a doubleton ace, king of clubs and he had bid one notrump, so he wasn't likely to have another doubleton. No, I placed him with three spades. But,' went on the Rabbit, 'as the Hog is always telling us, you don't win because you play well, but because opponents play badly. Give them every chance to go wrong. They won't miss them all.'

The Rabbit chuckled as he continued. 'Suppose, I thought, that Karapet had three spades to the jack, ten. Would he go up with an honor if I led the four of spades? After all, he didn't know that I had the eight and nine, so he might play low and then dummy's seven would force out the king.'

'But it didn't, did it?' I interposed.

'True,' agreed R.R. 'Papa won with the jack, so now my only chance was another mistake by the defense. Unless Papa had the ten of spades, as well as the king, he might not cover the queen of spades. Come to think of it, why should he?'

'But he did cover,' I objected, 'so no one made any mistakes at all, but you scooped Karapet's ten of spades, bringing off what's known as intra-finesse, though that was the last thing you had in mind.'

'Whatever you call it,' rejoined the Rabbit testily, 'it worked. Have it your own way. No one made any mistakes except me, but I made the contract.'

I hastened to agree. 'You did very well, and yet, without wishing to be pedantic, I don't quite see how you placed those spades round the table. You assumed correctly that Papa had three and you hoped to find Karapet with three more, the jack, ten deuce, to be precise. That would make fourteen spades in all, wouldn't it?'

'The trouble with all you experts,' retorted the Rabbit with spirit, 'is that you can't see the wood for the trees. You count everything all the time and all your figures are right, of course — except for the total. I'm no result merchant, as you know,' concluded the Rabbit, 'but when all's said and done, it's only the final number that counts, isn't it.'

Master Point Press on the Internet

www.masterpointpress.com

Our main site, with information about our books and software, reviews and more.

www.masteringbridge.com

Our site for bridge teachers and students — free downloadable support material for our books, helpful articles, forums and more.

www.bridgeblogging.com

Read and comment on regular articles from MPP authors and other bridge notables.

www.ebooksbridge.com

Purchase downloadable electronic versions of MPP books and software.